MAZE
A SHORT STORY COLLECTION

BY
JENNIFER JUNEAU

ROADSIDE PRESS

Maze
Copyright ©Jennifer Juneau 2024
ISBN: 979-8-3304-2121-3

All rights reserved. Printed in the United States of America. No part of this text may be used or reproduced in any manner without written permission from the author or publisher except in the case of brief quotations embodied in critical articles and reviews.

This is a work of fiction. Names, characters, places and incidents either are products of the author's imagination or are used fictitiously. Any resemblances to actual persons, living or dead, or actual events is purely coincidental.

Editor: Michele McDannold

Roadside Press
Colchester, IL

For my Mother

CONTENTS

If a Tree Falls 1
From a Room Above a Mexican Café 13
The Day Before I Died 17
Fast Food Horrors 26
Eight Days with the Yakatori Sisters 58
Broken 89
Nipple Knows Best 96
Smoking 102
Blind Date 109
Prelude to the Afternoon of a Faun 113
Isabel B. 129
Film Noir 142

Publication Notes 148
About the Author 151

"Good fiction's job is to comfort the disturbed and disturb the comfortable."

—David Foster Wallace

IF A TREE FALLS

If a tree falls in a forest and nobody is around to hear it, does it make a sound? This is the question my older brother Trey, who was flipping through a psychology magazine that belonged to our father, posed to my six year old self in our den one day in my childhood home. I didn't answer him, as I went on coloring in my Puff 'n Stuff coloring book, but I pondered the answer to that question, and what it meant, my entire childhood. I thought of ways I could find out: I would plant a tape recorder in the woods one stormy night and come back the next morning and by pushing the "play" button, see if the fallen tree had made a sound. Or, I'd simply venture out into the forest and hide behind another tree, a seemingly sturdy one, so that the falling tree wouldn't see me, and listen. I thought I was so clever. After a while I forgot about it and it wasn't until I took a psychology class in high school many years later that I learned the answer to that question was No. But that didn't stop me from constructing the idea. For example, last winter my mother, who I began calling Sylvia, phoned to tell me that my brother Trey had died. I had moved overseas to study art at Université de Lausanne and although I was devastated at Sylvia's pathetic assertion that my brother was dead, I didn't fly back to America for what she said was to be his funeral. I wouldn't. I wouldn't because I had no proof he was dead. Translation: If someone close to you dies because somebody told you that they died, even if you read it in the newspaper, but you never saw the body, are they really dead? My answer, of course, was No. Trey was alive. He just lost my phone number and my e-mail address and I couldn't reach him. As a matter of fact, if I Googled him this very minute all of his reviews and credits to his name would pop up on various websites as they always have: "Trey Waterman, Executive Chef and owner of The Coolest Cafe in L.A., was awarded one Michelin star…" and so forth. Nowhere would it say he hanged himself.

This past summer Sylvia had gotten some crazy notion that *I wasn't right.* Whatever that meant to her *I wasn't sure.* Nothing was further from the truth, because at thirty-nine I was feeling happier than I had in years. I began dating my art teacher, Jean Pierre, who was ten years younger than me. I suspected that Sylvia wasn't right because whenever I inquired about Trey, if she knew why he refused to phone or e-mail me lately, or if she thought that he couldn't forgive me for that awful thing I'd done to him, she would become silent. Maybe I'd frightened her somehow. I wouldn't ask about my brother's whereabouts in a calm manner, but I'd screech at the top of my lungs, obscenities included, right into her ear. I could picture her shaking her head to dispose of all those dirty words while her fingers moved to escort the words out. Then she'd come back on the line in a low tone, which actually frightened *me* and say slowly, "Isabel, I think you ought to come home for a while. *I don't think you're right.*" Then she'd start to cry. At that point I'd hang up.

Time couldn't pass without mileage, and my father, who was a clinical psychologist, died of heart failure at sixty-three. I was six and Trey was ten. I took his death hard. Although my father left us a fortune, Sylvia, who was in her forties, worked long hours at the local newspaper. She made a modest salary and socked it away into our trust funds which I later used to leave the country. Trey and I seemed fine without her, but like any biddable object I lumbered for stability. Trey was my sturdy tree. Never would he have guessed that one day I'd pay him back by screwing up his life.

When Sylvia phoned in late July, she told me she'd purchased a round trip ticket to come visit me since I wouldn't go back to the States. I was surprised. All I thought was, *There is a name and a face racing far from somewhere toward me.* Jean Pierre and I had already planned to go on holiday to the French Riviera where he had a home, and he suggested that Sylvia join us, she might enjoy lazing on the beach. His daughter Charlotte (a precocious four-year-old who had a command of three languages which included French, Italian and English) was visiting him for those two weeks—she lived with an aunt, or something, so he figured it would be a good opportunity for her to practice her English. If I agreed it was only to please him. I could have done with a summer without my mother.

The evening before Sylvia's arrival, I surveyed my flat. There wasn't much to fix, she'd only stay the night anyway since we'd be leaving for France the next day. I lit a joint. My brain was a serenaded field, reigning high all over the place. Feeling home-heavy, I took a walk. When I got back, my nerves were stilled and I slept so well I woke up late. I hurried to get dressed, find my wallet, my keys. Sylvia's flight would be arriving at four o'clock and I managed to get myself in the car in an attempt to avert traffic. When I arrived, I saw her at the airport gate, and noticed she had aged considerably. She looked around while the other passengers passed her rapidly, seemingly on their way to important places. A surge of anger tore through me, but I was baffled as to why or what I was angry at and concluded that every time I saw Sylvia I didn't know how not to be angry. I didn't call out her name, I watched her for a while and a part of me hoped she would walk past me and continue her journey with some other woman. There was no telling what preposterous tale she would spin under one roof, and in between four walls, once she got me alone. But she found me. And when she did she gathered my face in her hands and squeezed it so hard I must have turned blue. Through clenched teeth I offered to take her to a café for dinner. She obliged. There was not much she could do to me in a public place, so I assumed my mother's urges to drill Trey's death were kept at bay throughout eating cheese soufflé and pastry. In the end, she was too tired to shoot and by the time we got home, jetlag kicked in and she slept like a baby. Through the night I sat by my window, smoking cigarette after cigarette until dawn. When Jean Pierre pedaled up on his bike with his daughter and two backpacks intact I thought, *How perfect. Now rain will come.* It is that sweet scent mixed with herbs that accumulates in the air. Just as you stretch your arms up to the sky and take a deep breath, some evil god spits in your face. And so our day began.

They all sat on the front steps, bread and coffee in hand, including Charlotte who looked like a midget in lipstick, watching me struggle to load my Volkswagen with everyone's bags. Sylvia didn't want me to drive. I didn't have a choice since Jean Pierre didn't have a driver's license. Jean Pierre sat in the passenger seat and Sylvia and Charlotte were all snug in the back with books, paper and crayons. I turned the car over several times before we sputtered down the motorway to the border of France. Sylvia was sitting directly behind Jean Pierre, so every time I looked in the rearview mirror, I caught her staring at me. Her features took on the appeal of an old doily, yellowed and brittle. She made me nervous, and I thought, *I am a child killer yes, but I am no murderer.* I shook. I pulled the car over and took Charlotte out and told her to switch places with Sylvia.

There's only so much you could do to entertain a small child on a long road trip. We offered Charlotte carrot sticks because she was on a diet. We found playgrounds at rest stops, which I hated because it detained us. But Charlotte was bored and she wouldn't stop chanting the Are-We-There-Yet? chant which was an old standard among restless seat-belted children. Then we hit traffic.

"Why don't you color something for me Charlotte?" I suggested. "Or play tic-tac-toe with Sylvia?" She was all fidgety and Sylvia did nothing to entice her to play any game. She sat resting upon her elbow, staring out the window at nothing. I glanced in the mirror and saw Charlotte nudge her.

"Let's play hangman," she said.

"I don't like that game, Charlotte," Sylvia said.

"Why not?" she said.

"Because I don't," Sylvia retorted. I didn't know much about Charlotte, but I did know something about four-year-olds. They were persistent.

"Why not?" Charlotte wouldn't let up.

"Tell her why, Isabel!" Sylvia shouted up to me.

"Tell her what?" Jean Pierre whispered to me.

"I don't know," I whispered back, pretending not to know what Sylvia thought my brother did. Instead, I tried to distract Charlotte, since Jean Pierre believed in letting Charlotte be Charlotte by never getting involved in Charlotte's conversations.

"Charlotte, why don't you read Sylvia the book I gave you?" I said.

"Because I want to play hangman."

"Sylvia doesn't fancy hangman, Charlotte," I said. I wanted more than anything for everyone to get along. But the circle started again.

"Why not?"

"Make her stop, Isabel." Now, if I could make anyone do anything I'd make Sylvia disappear, and just as I was about to try (to make Charlotte stop) Charlotte said to her again, more sinister than innocent because now this was a game, "Why don't you want to play hangman?" and then Sylvia turned animalistic and crossed a border of her own accord and blurted out in a pitch high enough to deafen everyone in every car sentenced to this hellish standstill,

"Because my son hung himself!" The word "hung" bobbed in the air before it went limp, even *It* didn't want to be in that car. I shook my head slowly. Jeez, I thought. I was not a good sport when it came to practical jokes, but all kidding aside, her grammatical blunder is what pissed me off most. It's "hanged" not "hung" but I let that go and we drove on in silence because everyone was terrified now and cars started to move. I was certain Charlotte didn't understand the concept of one being "hung," nonetheless I was stung with fury at Sylvia's impetuous barking and as far as I understood it, Charlotte no doubt finished the statement in her head as "And if you don't shut up little girl, I'll hang you too." Substitute slap or kill for hang. I'm sure the verb didn't matter, it sounded like a threat. Jean Pierre looked at me and put his hand on my lap. He knew I had a brother. I never told him he was dead because he wasn't, but I didn't think he wanted to go there. Not yet, not in that car. So we continued to drive with Charlotte stunned into dumbness. I turned the radio on and made small talk with Jean Pierre.

In his French accent and half baked English he said, "Your mother, she feels, incinerated, yes?"

"Burned?" I knew what he meant, he was always mixing words up in an overzealous effort to expand his English vocabulary. "Do you mean incarcerated? Imprisoned in this car?"

"Is what I said."

When we arrived at the holiday house, it was past five o'clock and my car conked out two blocks from the driveway. The weather was overcast and people were already clearing the beach. After schlepping my duffle bag and Sylvia's suitcase in the heat (Jean Pierre was chasing after a speedy Charlotte) we settled in the living room with a bottle of wine. Charlotte ran up to her bedroom and wouldn't come out until Jean Pierre promised either to get rid of Sylvia or to open an account for her on the social networking site her pre-school used.

"Which site is it? My Face? Space Book? Because you know, the public has access to—"

"Face Space," Jean Pierre interrupted, not looking up from his laptop. "And it's enviously safe." Charlotte came downstairs with photographs of her Bratz collection that she wanted her father to post. She wouldn't go anywhere near Sylvia, who had gone upstairs to unpack. When I went up to help her, she was sitting on the bed staring out at the sea. She tried to tell me something, something about getting me help. About knowing I didn't mean to kill Trey's son. That it was an accident and everybody knew it was an accident. Her words were scattershot. Blah, blah, blah, and for me to stop feeling guilty, blah, blah, blah, about Trey's suicide and that's when I tuned her out and all I thought was, *You don't know what you're saying.* Her mouth moved but I couldn't hear a thing. She became a tree. A broken one. She continued to fall and fall and when she hit the bottom, although I was there, she didn't make a sound. My first instinct was to flee, as I did to Europe weeks after that ill-fated day my car lost its brakes killing Trey's only son. The death tore him and his marriage apart. I became a prisoner in my own home. My reclusive behavior rivaled my brother's pain until finally, as he sought therapy to deal with the death of his son, I became more depressed for causing it. Painting in a foreign country where I knew the language and wore my body thin and sickly was the only life I knew. Then at the suggestion of his psychologist, Trey finally found me. He phoned. He e-mailed. And just when I was convinced he'd forgiven me, all communication stopped.

So what? People lose touch all the time. But I was convinced he was still in this world and of it.

I walked over and stood by the window looking out into the haze. The sun broke through the clouds and out burst the inevitable downpour. The waves whipped in the wind and I opened the window to let the sound in because I had to crack the silence that winced in the background. The moment gathered like warm ocean around my ankles. I told myself, *If you want to keep it, you must wade further in.* Although the moment was not entirely mine, it was mine enough. I was seconds ticking and had to find the door that has kept me wide-open.

That moment turned to ice and I was the genetic makeup of its precipitation, stilled and thinking, *What brought me here in the first place?* How shiftless I'd become in all my dissolve! Because that moment couldn't run any faster if I chased it. Because that moment was already gone.

FROM A ROOM ABOVE A MEXICAN CAFÉ

If the walls could write books, what will start as love stories will end as tales of ineluctable heartache. If the walls could speak, they'd say he'd hold her close in a room redolent of must and lust. A world away from the spotlights and money so plentiful it could choke on itself, his fans, hollering for more, giving him a rush. Not to mention the uppers and the downers. The booze. Women. *Make it go away*. What these piss-stained walls would say. That the man was tall, dark-haired, and so sure of himself even the room fell in love. The woman was brunette. She'd be excited. He'd tear off her expensive silk with his teeth. The various sexual positions. The cries from this woman were of ecstasy, sometimes pain. The man was hard to read. According to the world, he was a hero. In his eyes, he was a failure. His worth as a man was measured by his ability to be adored, to make music, to make money.

To fuck in a rundown rented room with creaky floors, damp rugs and the occasional cockroach crawling up a wall in lieu of a palace-like hotel suite. The perfect backdrop to ease anxiety: the assumption of a perfect life put to rest.

Maze

Shouts outside the bodega blistered in foreign tongues. Laughter, brawls, gunshots, screams. A woman's tortured cries from the street turned the brunette woman on. A slap in the face: the woman begged her lover to fuck her hard to the beaten woman's cries.

And her lover did. With each stroke he'd fuck his terrible life away. Each stroke there went another lie. Each sensual touch: The tongue. The nipple. The clit.

The walls would tell you that at other times it was a different man. His hair was long and blonde. His lady was a model, tall and thin. Her hair also long and blonde. She'd cry over someone who'd broken her heart. The man would attempt to wipe her tears. She'd tear off his clothes, *It's ok it's only a shirt.* He'd lift up her skirt. He'd enter her from behind, sometimes on the bed, sometimes against the door. He'd twist her blonde strands in his fist, yank them hard. This is what she liked. She never looked him in his face. The humid room with no air conditioner, the scent of fetid crustaceans and salty air clung to their moist bodies as they fell onto the stale bedspread. This gave them a carnal thrill.

When it was over, the dark-haired man would light a cigarette. He'd summon a squat Mexican from the bar to bring him a bottle of tequila and some olives.

When it was over, the blonde-haired man would light a cigarette. He'd summon a squat Mexican from the bar to bring him a six pack of Pacífico and tortilla chips.

In both instances, ice water and lime would be ordered for the lady.

In both instances, the man's life had been imploding for a long time.

Whatever drove these two couples to their trysts will be forgotten for a good hour or two. The Mexican was paid handsomely to keep his mouth shut, but actually the Mexican didn't care. He hardly spoke. He wasn't legal in this country and he existed in a world of his own. His wife was pregnant, again, which will add one more mouth to feed his family of six.

No. He didn't speak their language, not in reference to English or to Spanish, but the kind where he got his hands dirty. His problems were real.

Later, the couples will separate and return to

their significant others, who weren't significant enough. When the room is dark and empty, the walls will say: *Fuck each other all you want. I know nothing.*

THE DAY BEFORE I DIED

It happened after the summer I came off a prescription painkiller addiction. Everything scared me. I was afraid of night. Afraid of the neon light that shone beyond the village, beyond the rolling hills that stopped just before the heel of the Swiss Alps. Müller's Shreineri blinked its eyes in the distance, purple narrow-necked stars crushed with morning silver, the same sign that used to give me comfort, knowing that someone, or something else, turned to the outcast night with questions. Most of all, I was afraid of my beating heart. The one inside my chest that pounded one-hundred and twenty-five beats a minute in the middle of the night. It's never been this way! But as they say, once you've dabbled, the battle to quit continues for life. Drying up sucked. I'd been ruined for years by the excursion of trespassers but it didn't end there. I sought information about my babies, the ones I'd given up. Those off-white rascals I developed an infinite affection for four years ago when I complained to my doctor of a backache. The night they were inaugurated into my system, they became part of my diet. I was indebted to them. My personality took on a different hue from those oval-shaped magicians that alleviated anxiety, filling my veins with a warmth I couldn't obtain any longer from human arms. At first they lulled me off to sleep, then as time went on they kept me awake. As a graduate student, I needed time. There never seemed to be enough time to do research and write my thesis. Insomnia became not only tolerable, but pleasant. I'd spin and spin the hours away at my laptop. My work improved because the drug allowed me to concentrate for long periods of time.

When I went online, I found that this painkiller was derived from the poppy plant. Having been three months clean, I made my way to the Indian grocer where they sold products in bulk. I read somewhere that if a person ate enough poppy seeds they would test positive for having drugs in their system. Far-flung as it seemed, I was desperate. I didn't want to look suspicious, so I loaded my cart with ten bags of curry powder and a sack of Basmati rice. Then I found my prize hulking high up on a shelf above the rest: a large plastic bottle of poppy seeds. I bought a case because I wasn't sure how much would be enough. And so it began, I ingested over a dozen spoonfuls of poppy seeds a day. I threw them in pancake batter, cereal and salads. I devoured them straight from the bottle. The effect wasn't the subdued euphoria I used to feel, but there was definitely something there. All in all I found my fix. The problem was, I began to get fat. I flirted with the idea of using again. How easy it had been! In the past, I had it all figured out. I used to walk into a pharmacy on a Saturday and complain of excruciating back pain. I'd tell the pharmacist that my doctor prescribed ___ in the past and that if he'd just give me one bottle, I'd take two to help me sleep and call my doctor first thing on Monday morning. This always worked in the catholic cantons, but no pharmacist in the protestant ones would honor my request. I was given a lecture on the dangers of using prescription painkillers without a prescription. Maybe the catholic cantons trusted people? I wasn't sure. But I was sure not to hit the same pharmacy twice, and since pharmacies reared their heads on almost every street corner in every village, it would be years (I calculated) before I'd run out of places to try. Then I'd start my search again, hoping I wouldn't be recognized. Seeking out yet another doctor to prescribe the drug was out of the question. I'd need another x-ray, and x-rays were expensive.

I was hesitant to start again for two reasons. One, there was the guilt factor. Each time I'd walk out of the drugstore securing my stash, I'd feel guilty for lying. I'd deliberately try to strain my back for pain. Still. Those trusting people began to wear on my conscience. And two, I overdosed. One fateful night I was in the emergency room with the feeling that somebody tied a plastic bag over my head. I kept track of how many milligrams I took, but the drug had been building up inside my system. I absorbed it like an industrial sponge and had a bad reaction. Reliving that moment when my body almost elapsed into respiratory failure was enough to quit. And just as I thought I had the prospect of starting again licked, I began to taste it. I craved those pills like chocolate cake. Two years ago, before my boyfriend left me, I'd taste them every time we fought. After all the Fuck Yous and all the slamming doors, I'd be stunned into placidity when two gulps of water collided with two gritty caplets. Forget poppy seeds. I was lonely and only moving closer to the roses.

Saturday had risen like a slap in the face and the

bus was packed. I should have left my house earlier, but I hadn't fallen asleep until four in the morning. I opted for public transportation over taking my car to the drugstore to create the illusion that somebody else was responsible for driving me to my old habit. I was nearer to my destination, not because we were gaining kilometers to town, but because the craving grew stronger. My heart was set on the upcoming high and I couldn't turn back. In the seats in front of me, a teenaged girl argued with her mother. I knew the joy of not having daughters. I knew the pain. Truth was, I hated myself. The quickening pace of my thirst that defined panic sickened me: a mangy animal scrounging for drugs. Chipped raw by insomnia, red cowboy boots, a white T-shirt and blue jeans, I stood out like the American flag. I wondered how many dishonest people sat on that bus. Then I rationalized: I wasn't that bad. After all, I wasn't hurting anyone. Not like the housewife across the street who suffocated her two children last Christmas Eve. Or the racists in Geneva who beat up an immigrant from a third world country with a chainsaw in a McDonald's. No, I was a good girl. It was my body, I could do what I wanted.

Maze

The bus suddenly took on the clean medicated scent of a pharmacy. As it rolled to town I practiced my spiel: *Hello. Good day*...No, wait. It wasn't supposed to be a good day. I was in pain. I had forgotten my lines. It was getting late and my future tasted like the traffic we hit, putting us in a standstill. The stores were about to close and I hadn't gone to the ATM yet. As the bus driver eyed me in his rearview mirror, I was convinced he read my mind. It was a conspiracy, this crawling at a sluggish pace. The pharmacy was a cough in the distance. I became nervous. Everything was closed on Sunday, it was now or another week. I couldn't go six more days with poppy seeds. I didn't want herbal teas. My loot loomed like a thunderstorm hovering in the distance, on the verge yet unable to extinguish a drought. I panicked now, and didn't know what to make of myself reeling in this blue rotunda, swelling out of something troubled. I was not a happy ending. But neither was I a sob story. Not yet. I told the bus driver I was ill and exited the bus. I walked down narrow cobbled streets, past cafés where people sipped cappuccino and laughed. Could one survive on laughter? I wouldn't know. I wove through shoppers and cars until I reached my destination. The church bells chimed the closing hour as I crossed the threshold of the drugstore. I was safe. The pure scent enveloped me, and my lungs filled with ecstasy. I was their last customer and I chanted in my head: *Though I walk through the Valley of the Shadow of Death I will fear no evil for Thou art with me.* Yes, I thought, as I hobbled to the woman smiling at the counter, my left hand supporting the small of my back, it was that easy. I launched right into it. "Do you have ___? I was up all night with back pain and, ohhhh…."

"Do you have a prescription?" And I thought: Yes, four years ago I had a prescription. I became so enamored by those little gems I ate them like candy. Now I go around from pharmacy to pharmacy and lie through my teeth so I can support my shitty habit.

"No."

"I'm sorry," she began, "but I cannot give you that without a prescription. We're closing now. Is there anything else you need?" *Yes*, I thought, *a gun*.

"Please, I was up all night. My doctor gives me these because they help me sleep. Monday morning, I'll see him." There were advantages of being a foreigner, or so I was told. People here tended to think in America you can get anything, anytime you wanted and we Americans were used to that. I began to believe it, as the druggist gave me a sympathetic look and disappeared into a back room. Then she emerged with the bottle.

"Just take two and drink a lot of water. Anything else?"

"Yes!" My enthusiasm startled her. She was tapping her foot. I whispered, as if I suddenly had a sore throat, "Green tea."

She placed the tea next to the bottle on the counter and rang it up. "Fifteen fifty."

I opened my backpack, rummaged through papers and books, reached for my wallet, which felt extra light, and then I was smacked with the realization that I hadn't gone to the bank. In all my manic fury to get to the store on time, I skipped the bank. All I had was an American Express card and they took only Visa.

"I, I—" I couldn't believe it. She watched me go through my backpack again. My arms and shoulders began to itch.

"I don't have any money," I said. And I thought: Don't look at me like that. Give me a long lecture about the dangers of drug use until the cows come home. Please say you trust me, that you know I'll be back Monday with the money. Just don't say No.

"I'm sorry," she said firmly, "if the pain is that bad, you might want to try the hospital."

In her haste to close up, she disappeared behind a curtain. I stood frozen for a moment, and as I turned to go, I noticed that the bottle sat next to the tea on the counter. I wasn't a thief. I never stole anything in my life, save a block of Bazooka bubble gum at a 7-Eleven when I was four, and I wasn't about to start. Because I'd pay her. I'd run to the bank and come back after dark and slip the money in the store's postbox.

The clock struck the quarter hour. As I sat on the bus, things began to happen. I leaned my head against the window and began to dream. There was a baby, dead, at the bottom of a swimming pool. I rescued it and blew air into its blue lungs. It sprang to life and I put her in a warm crib, where she sang in her own dry bed nursing water. There was so much to look forward to, her need for me grew. Then suddenly collapsed into the absence which I woke to.

Maze

FAST FOOD HORRORS

"Reality shows are all the rage on TV at the moment . . . but that's not reality, it's just another aesthetic form of fiction."
—Steven Soderbergh

The restaurant had been empty for months. We turned on the TV set that was fixed to the wall and channel surfed until we found what we were looking for. Margot, Patsy, and I had plenty of time to watch *Fast Food Horrors*. The reality show starred Celebrity Chef Gordon R. Crank. Crank was a big shot. An ex-footballer from the UK, he was built like a tank and had more energy than a truckload of Red Bull. When he quit the sports profession over a sprained ankle, his teammates walked off the field with him, and together they opened a diner out of the blue. Crank tried his hand at cooking and took the culinary world by storm with his signature breakfast dish: a scone topped with a duck egg. A cookbook, *3 Minute Breakfasts*, followed. After he became famous he ditched his staff, sold the diner, and opened a fast food place in the United States. He became head chef and owner of *Crank's Donkey Burgers* and was the first cook to be awarded three Michelin stars for a burger joint, which reportedly sold hamburgers at one-hundred dollars a pop (one-hundred and fifty with cheese and two-hundred for the Super Donkey—a burger with lettuce, tomato and pickle.) In *Fast Food Horrors* Crank shared his secrets of success with failures of the fast food industry. He'd barge into their businesses and tell them how to run it. When Crank spoke, people listened. His show was inspiring, as he'd materialize out of the sunset from coast to coast, and arrive on the troubled scene.

In college, Margot, Patsy and I were inseparable. Three years after graduation, our dream to be part of the trend and open our own fast food restaurant was realized. We pooled together our graduation money, and with help from Margot's father, we bought a seedy place in east L.A. because it was cheap.

We subsequently found a teenage runaway, a Mexican named Gonzalo Gonzalez, hanging out at the beach. He had chiseled features and grit that belied sensitivity. Patsy fell for him instantly. Gonzalo chain-smoked and wore a red bandana around his head. He spoke no English, but Patsy was fluent in

Spanish. We never dug into his past, but we took him under our wing and crowned him our head chef. In lieu of paying him, we let him live in the cellar of the restaurant.

We named our place *Burger Without a Bun* because it specialized in burgers without buns. Salad and celery sticks or lime Jell-O were offered on the side. Since modern day consumers were obsessed by cutting carbs out of their diets, we figured people would be more inclined to frequent our restaurant than any other burger joint in town, and they did. *Burger Without a Bun* was deemed the It Girl of burger places according to someone's high school newsletter. But now, three years later, it was yesterday's news.

In the *Fast Food Horrors* episode that aired that day, an Italian immigrant named Guido operated a fast food pizzeria called *Guido's*. The place boasted a kids menu box of mini fried pizza with a side of mozzarella sticks and a milkshake. After ten faithful years of sweating over deep fat fryers, Guido was losing profits and customers. Chef Crank paraded up the cobblestone walkway in a wealthy New England town that was as remote as a snowstorm compared to the crap neighborhood where *Burger Without a Bun* resided. He entered *Guido's* and took a look around.

"Ghastly," he said in his breathy Brit accent. Margot let out a breath of disgust, and Patsy and I couldn't take our eyes off the brawny bloke who was a ray of sunshine and hope in the ramshackle setting. He approached the counter and ordered the signature kiddy meal from the cashier, Gabriella, the teenage daughter of Guido. She nearly wet her pants at the sight of him. For us, his expert opinion on the grub was the focus of the show. We loved to watch other restaurants produce the same tasteless crap that we produced.

Crank poked the pizza with his index finger. The crust was petrified, he confided to his viewers, and the topping was cold and goopy. The bag containing the mozzarella sticks was grease-stained, and the milkshake was sour. As he glared into the camera, we knew deep in our hearts that he was speaking to us.

Crank saw enough. He summoned Gabriella to his table. She sauntered over with bells on. He insisted that she touch and taste the food. She picked up a limp mozzarella stick, held his gaze, and took a bite. He handed her the milkshake and said, "Now wash it down with this." She sucked the creamy liquid through a straw.

"Gross," she said, wiping her mouth with the back of her hand.

When he approached the Italian owner, Guido himself, Crank let loose. "You *bleeping bleep*," said the television set, "what the *bleep* are you running here?"

Guido, dumpy with broken English, defended his food. As usual our hero got the upper hand. He ransacked the refrigerator like a crazy man on a mission, eggs cracking onto the floor, and picked up a tub of what looked like mounds of cellulite. "What the *bleep* is this?" he said. At first Guido pretended he had no idea where it came from. Then we learned the contents of the sauce were full fat mayo mixed with mascarpone and lard. After Guido deep fried the pizza dough, he would slather the sauce on top, cover it with processed cheese slices and throw it in the microwave. The television set was on a tear.

"How could you *bleeping* serve this *bleeping bleep* to children?" The camera honed in on Gabriella, standing nearby, horrified, as she covered her mouth with her hands.

"Oh, sure," Margot said to the girl in the TV set, "like you didn't know?"

Guido told Chef Crank to go *bleep* himself and Chef Crank told him he'd gladly go *bleep* himself after he gave Guido a piece of his *bleeping* mind. Crank and Guido exchanged expletives like a string of firecrackers going off, and Crank slammed Guido up against a wall. Fretful music thrashed in the background as a narrator told us to stay tuned.

Gonzalo emerged from the basement with a cigarette dangling between his lips. He pulled up a chair in time to witness Chef Crank storm out the back exit of *Guido's*. As predicted, he returned that evening dressed in his whites. Guido was obliging because he wanted Chef Crank to buy him a ton of cool stuff. Not only did Guido cop a new brick oven, Chef Crank handed him his recipe for pizza sauce made from sundried tomatoes and capers. "Now," he said to Guido, "you can charge your customers a *bleep*load more."

After *Guido's* successfully hosted a kindergartener's birthday party, Guido gave Crank a rugged man hug to thank him. Patsy handed us tissues. Crank marched off into the starry night after one hour of inspections, revamping and bleeps. The happy ending caused our hearts to plummet: the television restaurant recovered and *Burger Without a Bun* remained sick. In an offhanded remark that must have been expressed dozens of times throughout the season, Patsy said, "I wish Chef Crank would fix our place."

Margot was inspecting her manicured nails; then her head shot up. "Why not?" she said.

We'd found our solution. Chef Crank would put *Burger Without a Bun* back on the map.

It was rumored that Chef Crank secretly harbored a degree in psychology and fixed personal issues between staff. It wasn't fact, but it was plausible according to what we saw. Not only would a reality TV show put us back on the map, it would mend our unwell friendship. I sought excuses that caused our collapse. Brainless acts. We'd freeze the burgers causing the flavor to relent to cardboard, and the oil in the fryer was never changed. We never ate our food. We'd take out Chinese from across the street because it was better. Our place was a shit hole, but it had always been a shit hole. In the past it brought customers in, so it's not like the walls suddenly deteriorated. But Margot was parsimonious to the extent of ruin. Blame Margot—she ran the show. In the three years since she graduated from UCLA, you'd think she would have developed business savvy.

SHAX network owned Chef Crank, so Margot went to their website and outlined our predicament in the online application. She uploaded a photo of the three of us—a daisy chain of damsels in distress in front of *Burger Without a Bun* with Gonzalo on his knees at our feet. The SHAX network replied that they did not believe our situation was dire enough to warrant the help we'd requested compared to the hundreds of other applicants. However, since the show's ratings hit an all time low, they figured the scenario of three hot blondes and a Mexican boy who shacked up in the cellar of a burger joint was the elixir the ratings needed. SHAX warned us that if we did not comply with Crank's advice, the viewers would hate us. Not only would our business be screwed, but we'd probably get death threats on social networking sites because the national public liked Chef Crank better than they liked us. We'd have a crappier reputation than before, in which case we'd might as well file for bankruptcy or slit our wrists. They'd dispatch their messiah immediately.

Chef Crank was due to arrive in one week. Instead of tidying up the place, Margo sat on the beach tanning herself, and Patsy took off for a manicure and a pedicure. I slumped on the couch watching TV lest I'd burn my fair complexion, and Gonzalo's whereabouts were Gonzalo's business.

Unlike the sunny episodes we've seen, it was an overcast day. Margot, Patsy, and I waited outside for our knight in shining armor. He zoomed in on a motorcycle with the SHAX van trailing closely behind. Reality sank in: *Chef Crank was here* and for the next few days *he belonged to us.*

Two cameramen and the sound crew began setting up as Crank took off his helmet. Patsy flipped her hair around asking how she looked, and Margot rolled her eyes. "Oh please," she said, "he's human. He takes off his pants like everybody else." And according to some tabloids, way too often.

"I'm Mike," one of the cameramen said, "and that over there is Jim." Jim was adjusting his camera lens. "Just pretend we're not here," he said.

"Where's our script?" Patsy said.

"We don't have a script," Mike said. "This was a last-minute gig."

Mike stepped aside as Chef Crank made a beeline toward us. Jim followed him steadily, and suddenly we were rolling.

Chef Crank was larger in person than he was inside our TV set. He wore a black T-shirt and blue jeans. He didn't notice the façade, a brown disk painted on the window that was supposed to represent a burger. We introduced ourselves as Margot, Patsy, and Corey. He gave us each a hug and a kiss. He squeezed me longer than he should have by the look on Patsy's face. He smelled like toast. Celebrities smiling from the glossy pages of cookbooks don't come with a scent. People do.

"Whoa," he stepped back. "What are three sexy blondes doing owning a burger joint?"

Patsy's cheeks turned beet. "Why don't I take you inside?" she said in a tone I wanted to punch.

"My God," he said, "this place really is a shit hole."

A red bandana tied around his head, Gonzalo was leaning back in a chair, cigarette in his mouth, watching *The Real Housewives of Spanish Harlem*.

"What's that?" Crank said.

"That's Gonzalo," Patsy said, "he's our head chef. He speaks no English, and he works for free."

"Wow," Chef Crank said. "Wow, wow, wow."

All Chef Crank wanted to do was eat. Cameraman Jim stayed with him and Margot stood at the register. Patsy, Gonzalo and I clunked about the kitchen in front of cameraman Mike. Mike asked me what I thought of Chef Crank.

"I have no idea," I said. "I just met him."

Patsy pushed me aside. "I have one word to describe Chef Crank," she said into the camera. "Hot. Hot, hot, hot." I got it. If the women in the previous episodes wrote the script, Patsy transformed into an actress. Mike gave her the thumbs-up.

From the kitchen, I watched Chef Crank grab a seat by the window with a view of a deserted laundromat. The menu was a series of snapshots of food that Margot took with her phone.

"Look at this menu," he said, loud and clear. "One crappy photo after another." He ordered a burger and a salad with celery sticks and Jell-O. In other words, he ordered everything. I handed Patsy a frozen burger, she handed it to Gonzalo, and he tossed it into the hot grease. While it sizzled Patsy and I chopped putrid bits off wilted lettuce and arranged it on a paper plate with sliced tomatoes. We scraped brown strings off celery sticks with a potato peeler until the sticks were as thin as Q-tips. The Jell-O took care of itself. When the burger made its way from fryer to plate, we threw the celery sticks on top for decoration and fit the Jell-O cup on the side. Patsy served it to Chef Crank with Mike on her tail. Chef Crank picked up a celery stick and sniffed it. He prodded the hamburger patty with a plastic fork while Patsy stood by his table. Margot spied from behind a rubber palm tree, and Gonzalo and I peered over the kitchen counter within earshot.

"Bloody hell," he said to the camera, as he poked the burger. "Looks like a hockey puck." He cut a piece and popped it into his mouth. His face twisted, and he took Patsy's palm and held it inside of his. She flashed him her scintillating white teeth. He spat the burger out in her hand. "This," he said, holding up her palm, "is a piece of shit." He threw the burger against the wall. The rubber tree shook its fake fronds. He scooped the Jell-O from its cup with a plastic spoon and it wobbled onto his lap.

"Fuck me," he said. He squished it into his mouth and spat it back on the floor and hacked. "Tastes like cough syrup."

Crank called each one of us to his table. Four morons stood facing him as he went off like a Roman candle. Yes, the cooking oil was spoiled. Yes, the place was a dive. Yes, the food was coated with freezer burn. The wilted lettuce, the rotten celery, and of course the Jell-O was shite—need he say more? But all this wasn't on top of Chef's agenda. The shocker was this: "This," he picked the patty up off the floor and waved it in our faces, as if we'd committed a crime, and then we learned we had when he said, "is not beef." It isn't? What is it? "This," he said, spitting flames, "is porridge mixed with breadcrumbs." (Porridge in Brit meant oatmeal in our language.) His delivery was executed with eloquence. "What have you fucking twats done?" Margot swallowed hard, opened her mouth, and shut it when he screamed in her face. "What kind of business are you running?"

"I—I don't know what you mean," she said. Her bottom lip curled.

"You've cheated your customers, sweetheart." His face crinkled up, and he squashed the burger on the table. "You've been selling porridge!"

"How can that be?" Margot balled. "Are you sure?"

"Fuck me, yes, I'm sure!" Chef Crank had over 10,000 people working under him so he could smell horseshit from a mile away. "Why did you lure me here?" he said. "To take the piss out of me?"

"Honestly, Chef Crank," I said, "why would we do that?"

"Well, because," he said, "everyone is crazy for me and can't get enough, that's why."

Regardless of our craziness his input was critical. Chef Crank nodded to the crew. Then *Cut!* rang out. He had his makeup retouched; then we rolled again with Margot's tears.

"I'm here to help," he said, embracing her. Patsy tried desperately to cry too, but everyone ignored her.

Margot pulled back. "*Cut!*" she yelled. "I won't let the public see me cry. How do my eyes look? Do I have mascara dribbling down my face? Are my cheeks streaked black?"

"You can't yell 'cut,'" the production assistant said. "Only we can."

"Crank complains too much," Margot whined. "This is *my* restaurant."

"This is a television show," Crank said.

"He's the star," I said. "He's supposed to criticize us." I turned to him. "Right?"

"Do you know how many people will be watching me?" Margot said.

"They'll be watching me, darling," Crank said, patting his face lightly.

"I won't appear distraught," she said.

"You're supposed to appear distraught," the lighting tech said. "Then the viewers can pity you."

"I thought the viewers were supposed to hate her," Patsy said.

"They were supposed to hate her," Mike said, "but this is the part where they're supposed to like her." He turned to Margot, "So keep crying."

"I can cry," Patsy said. "Can't they pity me?"

"Let's roll."

This was the scene where Chef Crank would interrogate us in a corner booth, and Patsy would admit that she made the burgers from oatmeal mixed with bread crumbs in an attempt to screw Margot. Patsy turned to her. "You're always in the spotlight, and I'm sick of it," she said. "Wait," she said to Mike. "Can I do that over?"

"What?" Crank said. He looked at Mike. Mike stopped filming.

"This is the last time we cut," he said. "Keep talking and we'll chop what we don't want during postproduction."

"OK roll," Patsy said. She cleared her throat. "You're *always* in the *spotlight*."

Chef Crank could give a shit about anyone's spotlight. Once he had his information, he went into the kitchen with Gonzalo to rummage through the freezer because that was next in the schedule, and shooting could go on for hours. Both cameramen followed them.

At the table Margot confronted Patsy. "Oats? Spotlight? What's wrong with you?" She turned to me, "Did you know about this?"

"Pipe down," I said.

"It's starting again," Patsy said.

"What's starting again?" Margot said. She looked at me. "I've got no clue what she means."

"Applying for the show was a mistake," I said. I turned to Patsy, "Oats?" I glanced at our pathetic menu. "This is embarrassing. I'm out of here."

"That's brilliant!" Patsy said. "How many people have walked out during the episodes we've seen and looked like assholes?"

"She's right, you should leave," Margot said. "Then Chef Crank will chase you down the street, and you'll look like one big asshole in front of the entire viewing world."

"He might even go to your house with the cameramen and tell you off," Patsy said. "What an episode!"

It was impossible not to make the same mistakes other people made on the show. How easy it was to pass judgment as a viewer—how often we'd say: How could that asshole walk out when Chef Crank is there to help? But when you're the victim of reality, you have to try hard not to be yourself.

"Wait," I said, "in exchange for a good episode, we should act like assholes?"

"No," Patsy said, "just you."

"Margot?" Chef Crank called, "can you come here, darling?"

Patsy and I followed Margot into the kitchen. "Yes, Chef Crank?" she said in her best TV voice, "what seems to be the problem?"

"Biff Wilson," Patsy said and crossed her arms.

Margot faced Patsy, "Buff? Wilson?" She searched her memory of years ago. "Who's Buff Wilson?"

"You could show me what's wrong, Chef Crank," my voice rose over the squabble.

"*Biff!*" Patsy said.

"The freezer is leaking water," Crank said. "The moisture is producing mildew."

"Phi Kappa Sigma," Patsy said. "Sophomore year? In the backseat of Biff's car? You didn't think I knew?" All trysts in the frat house whistled the same tune for Margot back then, and Patsy thought *Fast Food Horrors* was the place to discuss it.

"Your freezer is fucked," Crank said, as he dug deeper, pulling out rancid oat burger after rancid oat burger.

Patsy erupted and called Margot a whore and a slut. Crank's attention was arrested immediately. Margot and Patsy clawed at each other's hair like felines. Margot's chunky rings clanked against something, maybe against Patsy's chunky earrings. Chef Crank, forsaking all thoughts of restaurant rehabilitation, yielded to the display.

"Wow," he said as he tossed a burger onto the counter. "Wow, wow, wow." I wanted to jump in and stop them, but my arms wouldn't work, and I became entertained with the rest of the SHAX crew. The scent of deep fried nastiness lingered under my nostrils from Gonzalo's muggy breath as he leaned over my shoulder to watch the mess of you-slept-with-my-boyfriend-years-ago writhe on the linoleum. Four stilettos scratched against the puke-green tile creating marks on the floor. Their heels dug into each other's shins, and you couldn't have gotten a better show if you were at a mud wrestling match. It was easy to fall prey to a camera when you knew the public would be watching. But this was just the kind of scene that attracted me to reality TV, too.

To everyone's dismay time ran out, and Chef Crank and the crew had to shove off.

"Let's go for a drink," Margot huffed.

"Let me get my purse," Patsy puffed.

We went to a local bar and got drunk.

"What was that all about?" I said, sipping at an empty beer mug. I motioned for a refill.

"The crew loved it," Margot said, lighting a cigarette.

"This is turning out to be fun!" Patsy said.

"You've got to start doing something worthwhile for the show," Margot said to me.

"You want me to act?" I said.

"Well, duh," Patsy said, "we are on TV."

"What do you want me to do?" I said.

"Get really upset, like you care."

"I do care!"

"Television is a drug. The viewers are addicts. We're the suppliers," Patsy said. "If viewers get a good fix, we may even star on *Fast Food Horrors Revisited*!"

The next morning Chef Crank sat us down in a corner booth to relay his rumination of yesterday's inspection. I tried not to be myself.

"It will take a miracle for the community to trust you after deceiving them with porridge," he said, waving his finger in our faces. "But your food isn't the only issue." This was my cue.

"Oh, Chef Crank," I pleaded, raising my eyebrows, "we are *sooo* desperate. I mean, we'll do anything you wish. We, like, so dig you that it hurts."

"Corey, shut it," he said, "and I have just the expert who can help."

Maze

We braced ourselves for one of his specially trained chefs to enter, or top accountant, or a wicked cool food distributor. Chef Crank knew an expert in every pocket of the earth. And just when we thought we'd seen it all—God walked in. The big guy gave Crank a high-five. He eyed the place. His long ancient robe billowed in a sudden wind. He looked the camera in the face, fingered his beard, and led the way as he surveyed the eatery. We held our breath. If anyone had an answer to this mess, it would be him. Through God's eyes it was clear how much of a pigsty our joint had become. With his narrow finger he swiped the shelves that held our cheerleading trophies. It came up dust. He gazed at our cheerleading photos that Margot hung on the wall by a broken jukebox. The jukebox was old and was a gift from Margot's parents' attic. The only 45 that played was a Beatles one. We loved the Beatles, but it was a crappy B-side Ringo song. And it skipped. We never got around to fixing it. God put a nickel in and when the tune came skipping on, he looked up as if to ask himself, *Why?* Crank hurried over and hit the jukebox with his fist. God returned to the photos on the wall. He shook his head in distaste as he glimpsed a picture of me with my arms in a high-five position standing atop a row of football players. I watched the cameraman watch Crank as he watched God watching me. God walked toward the restrooms; then suddenly he tripped, landing on all fours. He stubbed his toe due to an uprooted chunk of tile that left a crevice in the floor. Crank gave us a look as he helped God up. God brushed himself off and continued to the bathroom and shut the door behind him.

"Look at what you imbeciles have done!" Crank yelled. "You'd be lucky—*lucky!*—if God could save you."

Patsy made the sign of the cross. I copied Patsy, and Margot was shell-shocked over the whole God thing because she is an atheist—excuse me, *was*. God took an extraordinary length of time in the toilet, so Crank went in to check on him. We huddled outside the Men's Room door peering in. There was no sign of God. The window had been flung open.

Crank snapped his fingers. "Ok, over there, twats." He sat us down in a corner booth after God escaped with no insight other than our business was in dire straits. "I'm gobsmacked," Crank said, shaking his finger at us. "Out of all the restaurants I've ever been in I've never, ever, seen such a disaster."

"What's 'gobsmacked' mean?" Margot said to Patsy.

"No idea," Patsy said. "Probably something horrid."

"It means 'shocked,'" I said, "in Brit."

"You're really in the shit," Crank said to Margot. "You've got fuck all." He'd said this to almost every owner in the episodes of *Fast Food Horrors* that aired. Gonzalo emerged from his pit, his baggy jeans slung below his boxers, with a bowl of oatmeal. He sat down. Margot shot Patsy a look.

"What's wrong with you?!" Crank said to Gonzalo.

"*¿Qué?*"

"How could you stuff your face with porridge in front of Margot after what Patsy did?"

"*¿Qué?*"

"The *burrrgers*, the *burrrgers*," Crank drawled. Gonzalo spooned oats into his mouth. "Me no English."

"Bloody hell," Crank said, "I'm about to quit."

Nobody said a word. Mike lifted his head over the camera and made a gesture for one of us to speak.

"Oh. Right." Margot cleared her throat. "Please stay." She looked at Mike. Crank rolled his eyes. Margot pretended to cry. "If I lose my business, I lose everything," she said and hung her head.

"So, like, should we give up?" I said. Watch—*Never*.

"Never," Chef said, "never, ever, ever, ever, ever. But you've got to work as a team."

"So, like, if we do whatever you say, then we won't be a bunch of losers?" Patsy said.

"No," he said, "you're still a bunch of losers. You'll just need to cooperate."

We promised him we'd cooperate from that point on. Mike gave us the thumbs-up behind the camera as Crank assigned duties for the relaunching of the restaurant. Patsy was to scrub the toilets and the sinks with her toothbrush, and Margot and I were to help Chef Crank paint the walls and retile the floors. Gonzalo was assigned the mission of spreading the word that Chef Crank was in town by visiting the Hispanic community and delivering flyers begging them to give *Burger Without a Bun* a second chance. Chef handed him flyers written in English and Spanish that guaranteed the best burgers that their customers would ever eat made from 100% beef. Margot threw her arms around Chef Crank. He clung to her joyfully. He liked to hug people. Especially people like Margot.

Chef Crank splurged for a new freezer, and the jukebox was replaced with an Xbox. The cheerleading photographs were blown up into life-sized posters. Chef sent Patsy down to the local slaughterhouse to see what hamburgers were really made out of, and two days later the place was brand new. The kitchen was stocked with minced cattle.

Chef Crank demonstrated how to cook hamburgers on the state-of-the-art grill he installed. He whipped up a recipe before our eyes: ground sirloin with Worcestershire sauce, chopped leeks, Dijon mustard, pickled beets and braised fennel.

"Pay attention," he said as he kneaded the meat. "Let me show you how it's done." We focused on his fingers, pushing slowly at first, then gradually pushing faster into the meat with his thumbs. "You've got to get deep in there," he said, looking at Margot. "Grind it." Gonzalo took notes. "The faster you grind," he continued, "the better it gets until the mixture comes together." Patsy let out a sigh.

He mounded the meat into balls, then squashed them between his palms and put them on the grill. "No more deep frying." He smacked Gonzalo on the chest with the back of his hand. "Got that, amigo?" He gave us a taste of the finished product.

"Umm," Margot said dramatically, wiping her lips, "party in my mouth." Patsy said it was amazing because that was her favorite word. I thought it needed salt, but I wasn't about to shatter any myth in front of the television viewers by saying so, so I ended up concurring with the group.

Our place was set to reopen at lunchtime. We waited until two-thirty, but nobody came. After all the effort we'd made, the relaunching of *Burger Without a Bun* did not bring in any business. News of Chef Crank's arrival brought no new customers as nobody in town had heard of Chef Crank. Nobody could afford to.

"We'll have to expand advertising beyond your borders," Crank said. He ogled us. "I have an idea, but there's somewhere we need to go first." He took Margot by the hand, and the cameramen followed. They hopped into the SHAX van and sped off.

"Geez, that sucks," I said. "How come we couldn't go?"

Patsy shrugged. "I don't know. Because we have to stay here and keep an eye on things."

"Like what?" I said. "What things?"

"I don't know," Patsy said. "Gonzalo."

"Is it because Margot's the prettiest?"

"No," she said, "don't be absurd."

"Yes, it is," I said. "Margot gives good television face."

"Save it," Patsy said. "Save your spiel for Mike and Jim."

"Girls, I have a surprise for you," Chef said when they returned. "Put these on." He pulled out sapphire hot pants and melon halter tops from the shopping bag Margot was holding. Margot took her set and held it against her body in front of the mirrored wall.

"Aren't they fantastic?" she said. "Chef bought us new outfits!"

"The colors will go amazing with my new boots!" Patsy said.

Chef Crank beamed. "Now you will stand out from your competitors!"

I wanted to die. There was no way I'd degrade myself by squeezing into hot pants. I hadn't been working out recently, and my figure was flaccid. But my resistance would send the "asshole threat level" to red alert, and my expression must have confirmed that because Mike and Jim zoomed in on me.

"Tell the viewers what you think, Corey," they said.

I wanted nothing more than to hold the clothes up and say, "Fuck these, fuck hot pants," but ended up saying something banal. "Thanks, Chef Crank, thanks an awful lot."

"No problem," he said. "Hey, where's Gonzalo?" He clapped his hands. *"¡Gonzalo! ¡Vamos!"*

We paraded the streets in our hot pants. We hopped buses from avenues littered with trashcans to boulevards littered with BMWs. Gonzalo and Chef Crank handed everyone who walked by a sample burger wrapped in lettuce, and Margot, Patsy, and I handed out invitations to a relaunch of our relaunch. Chef Crank took a poll, and most people said they'd happily pay a buck for our burgers. The men said they'd pay even more if we personally served them in our hot pants.

The crowd was posh, not one you'd normally see grace *Burger Without a Bun.*

"Isn't this amazing?" Patsy said. Japanese businessmen were lined up outside the door with their cameras ready to snap pictures, and I wanted to set fire to myself.

Margot smoothed down her hot pants. "Oh, look. A camera. Come." She pulled Patsy over to the side while Jim interviewed them.

Customers mulled about waiting to be seated. The smell of grilled wholesomeness emanated from the vents into the alley drawing locals in as well. Margot greeted each guest and took their orders. She checked on each table and worked the room, aware of Jim pursuing her. Mike filmed Patsy and me in the kitchen shaping burgers with the help of Chef Crank while Gonzalo grilled. If there was anything to prove, it was that we had learned to make decent food. As I scooped a handful of meat and began mounding it into a burger, I felt something hard and squeezed what I thought was a piece of pickled beet in between my thumb and forefinger, then flicked it into the trash. After the orders settled, Margot, Patsy, and I, as suggested by Chef Crank, stood waving to a cheering crowd of patrons. Chef Crank was about to usher in the mayor of the city to hand *Burger Without a Bun* the Best Bang for the Buck award. Food critics huddled together in a corner booth. Then a shriek came from the kitchen. The place fell silent.

"¡Cocinero! ¡Una cucaracha! ¡Cocinero!" Gonzalo tore out of the kitchen. *"¡Cocinero! ¡Muchas cucarachas!"*

A lady at one table asked what Gonzalo was yelling, and someone from another table whispered in her ear, and this went on from table to table like the telephone game until the end when the last patron exclaimed, "It's a rat!" A cockroach, a rat. What difference did it make? People spat their food out and began leaving.

"Chef Crank!" Margot yelled, "help us!" She turned to Mike or Jim, I couldn't tell them apart anymore, and said, "Stay tuned, America, Chef Crank will fix this."

We followed Crank into the kitchen as he ripped Gonzalo a new one, an old one, whatever the cliché. "You've made a wanker out of me in front of the American viewing public!" he screamed, waving his finger in his face. "After all I've done! Calling the mayor, sealing you an award." He shook his head.

"There are bloggers out there!" Gonzalo understood squat but kept wiping his face from Crank's spittle. Margot started to cry for real, her bottom lip quivering too much to yell *Cut*.

Roaches crawled across the sparkling countertops and filed into nooks and crannies as I tried whacking them with a dishtowel. One held its balance on the rim of the bowl that contained raw meat. The cameras followed Crank to the cellar, and Margot, Patsy, Gonzalo, and I followed the cameras. Crank switched the light on, and it turned out that the cellar, which was Gonzalo's living quarters, was infested with roaches and garbage. Nobody ever went down there because that would have been, like, invading Gonzalo's space. Gonzalo told Patsy that he didn't notice the roaches because the cellar was dark, and he only dropped to bed half drunk, but in retrospect while sleeping on his futon he felt creepy, itchy things crawling over his skin. As the roaches scurried under the lights, the SHAX crew took to their phones, relaying the scene with glee to whomever they relayed it to.

But the show mustn't always go on. After the diners left, Chef Crank walked out the door with the cameras behind him to where the lighting crew waited. This was the last scene. The one where he'd predict the outcome of our business. He'd walk off into the night, leaving our fate hanging in the balance. We'd have to wait several months for the episode to air while SHAX spliced us, diced us, superimposed us, set us to music and narrated us from their perspective.

The temperature dropped. Clouds dispensed rain. The crew packed their belongings, and Chef Crank came back in, shaking off the weather, not as a celebrity shooting a television show, but as a guy named Gordon, who happened to be an exquisite chef. We posed for photos. We bantered about Margot and Patsy's catfight, maybe about the oats. I can't remember. We idly put odds and ends back into their places. The rain stopped. One of us mumbled something about going out for a drink. Then suddenly, the events that transpired in the last few days didn't seem so important.

.

Maze

EIGHT DAYS WITH THE YAKATORI SISTERS

I hated supermarkets and everything associated with them. Even the sight of the coupon-laden circular each week threw me into a tailspin. I stopped watching television because supermarket jingles made me break into a sweat. But no matter how abstruse the aversion grew I found myself in a supermarket in a suburb of Boston not far from my apartment. An old college roommate was in town and since I used to cook the meals in our off-campus apartment, I wanted to reminisce with a dessert she loved. It required lychee nuts. Which is why I made a beeline to the fruit and vegetable section the minute I entered the store. I planned to go in and out under sixty-seconds flat. When I discovered that there weren't many lychees left I attempted to scoop them all in one handful but in my haste one fell and when I bent to pick it up a short man emerged out of nowhere and stood in front of the crate for what seemed an eternity. I waited as he stood inspecting what was left of the lychees. I broke into a sweat.

I wish I were magnanimous. I wish I were the type who concludes, Oh well, shit happens. But the ding-dong of the intercom followed by the grandiose voice announcing a two-for-one sale on chocolate pudding in aisle five pulverized my nerves and, didn't I say *Excuse me sir?* Maybe. Maybe the plea was inaudible or the man didn't understand English or he was a stickler because he didn't budge, so I muscled up beside him and gave him a sharp nudge in the ribs. He didn't flinch. I gave him another. Then he did. He bent forward to smell the lychees. He kissed them. He French kissed them and suddenly I was knocked aside by a lady, who I surmised was his wife, grabbing his shoulders, muttering something in his ear in an inexplicable tongue that got louder and louder and finally hysterical until I realized that the man was neither smelling nor kissing the lychees but having a seizure. His black rimmed eyeglasses fell to the floor and I picked them up. Then I yelled Help. I mean, I screamed it in a guilt-ridden I-am-a-good-person kind of way that said I would never bully any member of the human race who was blocking the food product I'd like to covet, especially if it turned out that he was an epileptic. Or had some other dormant disease that finally surfaced. A clever prepared-for-anything super mom with five kids in tow whipped out her cell phone and dialed nine-one-one. In the end, when the paramedics arrived and after the woman with the five children left, the wife approached me and thanked me for yelling Help. I handed her her husband's glasses and told her it was nothing, because it wasn't anything, and she said it was something and we went back and forth until I said, "If there's anything else I could do." Which there probably wasn't because she jumped into the ambulance with her stretchered husband. But then she tossed me her car keys, described the BMW in the first spot in the parking lot and told me to meet her at the general hospital. I stood, keys in hand, mouth agape. "The name's Yakatori," she said. The ambulance door slammed shut, sirens and red lights ablaze, and they were on their way.

As if I had nothing better to do on the first Saturday in weeks that the sun proved it still existed. Besides, what about my car? Didn't Mrs. Yakatori think of that? Even though I'd taken the tram shopping because I didn't own a car. Still, she didn't consider it. Then I considered this: this woman is frightened for her husband's health and here I am, an accommodating samaritan, inquiring if there was anything I could do, which people sometimes ask rhetorically, and she called me on it by saying Yes.

Not having driven a stick shift in years I bucked the Yakatori's BMW to the hospital through Boston traffic. When I arrived I found Mrs. Yakatori in the waiting room and Mr. Yakatori in a coma. "I don't understand it," she said, "he seemed healthy."

"Surely he had an illness?" I said.

"That's what the doctors are going to find out," she said, "but nothing I am aware of." I wanted to offer my well-wishes and take off like a hit-and-run but she handed me a slip of paper. "Here is my address," she said. I must have turned ashen because she said, "You asked me what you could do." She's right. I did. I looked at the address. She lived in a rich neighborhood a few blocks from my apartment. "I won't leave my husband's side," she said. Then it dawned on me: as when a neighbor is on vacation, I'd retrieve her mail. I'd water a plant.

"My name is Dora," I said. "What would you like me to help you with?"

"Go to my house tonight, Dora, and cook supper for my daughters." I wondered how old her daughters were. Old enough to stay home alone but not old enough to cook their own supper. "I will stay the night in hospital," she said. "Is it no trouble?"

"No trouble?" I snickered. "Shall I pack you a suitcase too?"

"Yes," she said. "And don't forget my toothbrush." A nurse approached Mrs. Yakatori and they became engrossed in conversation.

"Oh, Dora," she called over the nurse's shoulder as I was leaving, "I will phone my daughters to tell them you are coming."

I gave up cooking years ago after college when I gave up supermarkets. Nevertheless, I went. I went to Mrs. Yakatori's house in an attempt to cook her daughters supper to absolve myself from the diabolical act of nudging a man in the ribs who prolonged my miserable existence in the fruit and vegetable section at a supermarket. Especially now that the poor guy was sick.

I drove until I reached the block where the Yakatoris lived. Each colonial-style home debased my lifestyle. I pulled in front of the second to last house on the left. It was more prominent than the others with a circular driveway and two white columns at the front door. The Yakatori house was made of brick. The front door was painted red with a gold knocker.

An overnight bag waited by a wooden replica of a birdhouse which was their mailbox. On the mailbox roof stood a velvet bird with a note taped to its beak from the Yakatori girls asking me to bring the overnight bag to their mother. The girls had other arrangements for dinner, the note said, and for me to wait outside.

I waited and waited and waited for—what? I wasn't sure. Maybe they were cooking *me* something splendid to take away for comforting their mother. Then a pizza delivery truck pulled up.

"Are you Dora?" the delivery boy said.

"Yes," I said, "why?"

"That'll be thirty dollars," he said.

"I didn't order a pizza," I said.

"You are Dora, right?"

I nodded.

"It says on the delivery slip that Dora will be outside to pay for the pizza." He showed me the slip. It said that Dora will be outside to pay for the pizza. I automatically gave him thirty dollars out of what I can only describe as shock.

I had nothing left for a tip, and while the boy took the pizza to the red door I fled back to the intensive care unit with Mrs. Yakatori's overnight bag. She'd fallen asleep on a chair by Mr. Yakatori's bedside and I left the bag with a nurse. My old roommate called to say she'd managed to get tickets to the Boston Ballet for her and her daughter. She couldn't make it after all. I said I understood. Truth was, my head was still spinning with the Yakatori incident and I didn't care. Besides, I never did buy the lychee nuts.

* * *

Day 1 Sunday

I phoned the hospital first thing the next day to check on Mr. Yakatori. "Critical but stable," said the nurse. I rushed to the hospital to drop off their car.

When I entered the intensive care unit, I eyed Mrs. Yakatori and her daughters through a window. A rush of sadness washed over me. The two girls, about sixteen, held each one of their mother's hands. Instinctively, Mrs. Yakatori turned and her face elapsed into a smile. The girls turned too and they came to greet me.

"How's Mr. Yakatori?" I said to Mrs. Yakatori, handing her the car keys. "Did they find anything?"

"Not yet," she said. "Oh, these are my twins, Maya and Winona." I shook their hands. "I meant to thank you for the pizza, Dora. How much do I owe you?"

"Thirty dollars," I said. She went for her purse.

When she returned she didn't hand me money she handed me a map. "There is something else I need you to do, Dora." Tears welled in her eyes. "I cannot leave my husband," she said. She gently placed the car keys back into my palm. "Could you please pick my girls up tomorrow morning and take them to school?" I looked at the twins. They were so sweet in their matching floral sundresses! I thought, if I had twins I'd want them to be exactly like the Yakatori sisters. "Yes, of course!" I said. I was smitten. She added that if I could drive her daughters to school every day for as long as her husband would stay in the hospital, she would be grateful. The arrangement was this: she would hold vigil by Mr. Yakatori's bedside. I'd pick up the girls from their house at seven a.m., drop off Winona at art school on the way to the city, then drive Maya several more miles to the music academy in the city. Since the girls started and ended school at different hours, they would each take a tram directly to the hospital after school to visit their father. At which point, their mother would eat dinner with them at the hospital, then the girls would take the tram back home and Mrs. Yakatori would remain at Mr. Yakatori's bedside until the pattern started again the next day. I'd use their car. "OK," I agreed, "no problem." Compassion tugged at me. It was the least I could do.

"Any questions?" she said. I wondered why the girls can't take a tram to school. "I bet you wonder why the girls can't take a tram to school," she said.

"No, I don't," I said. "Honest."

I was not a morning person. I was a penury-stricken graduate student whose father still paid my tuition and rent and I should have completed my graduate degree years ago. I spent my nights studying and surfing the net. Besides, how long could anyone be detained in a coma?

I drove to the girls' house that evening to get to know them, at Mrs. Yakatori's request. As I downed a bacon cheeseburger and a box of onion rings on the way, I basked in the luxury of driving a car. As if taking respite from public transportation weren't enough, there must be compensation for driving the girls to school. I daydreamed that the Yakatoris were royalty in disguise and if I remained at their side until Mr. Yakatori snapped out of it, they'd pay me back in riches. Forget earning a graduate degree to find a well-paying job! I'd live on the Yakatori fortune and go on an expensive vacation. I'd buy a car. I was spending the reward money fast: I was the maiden in Aesop's fables who carried the eggs on her head while she daydreamed of fame and fortune. Only I wouldn't slip.

The living room was decorated in antiques with pillows strewn about, plants and Persian rugs. Winona served herbal tea and both girls told me about themselves. They were thirteen. They looked older and were brilliant. They both studied at private institutions on scholarship. Maya attended a music academy in Boston and Winona studied visual arts at an acclaimed college on the outskirts. Both girls were academically advanced for their age and I learned that their education was the reason why the family came to America. I sat in the middle of the two, Winona showed me her artwork while Maya showed me photographs of their home in Tokyo. I inquired what their father did for a living. They said their mother was the breadwinner, she owned her own business. The mood was jovial and I didn't want to leave—as I was a distraction from their father's grim predicament—but it was getting late.

"Well girls," I said, placing my tea cup on the coffee table, "I've got to go. You'll be all right?" They looked at each other and Winona nodded to Maya. Maya ran upstairs and Winona proceeded to show me out. "I'll see you tomorrow at seven," I said, "good night."

"Wait!" Maya rushed to the front door with two canvas bags and handed them to me.

"What's this?" I said.

"Our dirty laundry," she said.

"Laundry?" I looked at one twin, then the other. "You want me to do your laundry?"

"Yes," Maya said.

"Why can't you do it?" I said.

"Because we're thirteen," Winona said.

"We have better things to do," Maya said.

"Yeah," Winona said, "we have a life."

"But—"

"We're tired," Maya said.

"We're sad because our father is sick," Winona

said. "Good night." They shut me out. I had no time to think. I had laundry to do.

* * *

Day 2 Monday

The twins were fraternal, did I mention that? Which meant they didn't have to look alike. Which meant it was easier to tell the difference between them than if they were identical. It was as if they weren't twins at all! I'd be a moron if I mixed them up, which I must have been because I mixed them up once. OK, twice. Even though Maya the musician had jet black hair down to her hips and Winona the artist had short cropped hair with ferocious red stripes, I thought Maya was Winona and Winona was Maya the first morning I picked them up for school. They didn't say hello. They must have been tired because they were talkative last evening at their house. Both girls stood on either side of the car.

"The doors are unlocked," I said. They did nothing but wait until I opened the car doors for them. "One of you could sit up front with me."

"No thanks," they said.

The car didn't have a GPS.

"Why doesn't your car have a GPS?" I asked either one of them.

"Our father scorns technology," Winona said, "he's set in his ways."

"Besides," Maya said, "nobody likes being told what to do."

Both girls read books as we drove in silence until I dropped off Winona. Who I thought was Maya. Maybe I was the tired one. I was up all night doing laundry. First I was to drive to the spot on Mrs. Yakatori's map illustrating the first drop off point with a circled number one which was the art college for Winona. Next, I was to drive to the spot with a circled number two, which was the music academy for Maya. I was making conversation with whichever girl remained when I elapsed into a self-deprecating spiel about my dabbling in art for a semester back in undergrad school and how I had flunked. That nobody ever failed art, subjective as it was, and that I was the first student ever, my professor said, to get an F. I told the presumed Winona, as I referred to her as Winona throughout the conversation, or in this case I was conversing with the dashboard, that, from artist to artist, she could identify. Creative as I was, my work wasn't recognized—and—did she ever have a moment like that? I glanced in my rearview mirror to capture the fake Winona's reaction. There was a smirk on her face. Truth was, she was gloating as I humiliated myself. I mean, only an artist, a person studying visual arts, I stammered, could understand the trepidations of, well, failed art. When I dropped her off, I opened the door for her, as I did for her twin sister or else neither one would have gotten out. I gathered her belongings and handed them to her, said goodbye, and she said nothing except, "I'm *not* Winona."

Late that evening, out of curiosity, I checked to see if the Yakatori sisters were on Facebook. Their profiles were public. Maya's profile picture was a selfie. She wore a tight black dress to accentuate her stick thin figure and her face was heavily made up. Winona's picture was simply a collage of her artwork. I viewed their photographs and read their timelines. Some posts were in Japanese, some in English (many boys flirted with them and used expletives.) I watched links on YouTube of punk bands I never heard of, etc., etc., until I scrolled down on Maya's timeline to discover a status update that read, *If I ever become a garrulous middle-aged loser who knows squat about art, shoot me* of which received two-hundred and twenty-two "Likes." I was taken aback—was she referring to me? Number one, I wasn't middle-aged and number two, I wasn't garrulous. OK, I admit at times I am a walking run-on sentence. Still, I didn't mean to be garrulous to her. It was meant for Winona.

Winona's Facebook timeline wasn't as offensive—she may have been the nicer twin, I may be wrong. I logged out before I'd have a chance to find out.

* * *

Day 3 Tuesday

I tried to get those girls to like me. I bought them croissants Tuesday morning. I scraped up change I found in jeans' pockets (jeans belonging to them of which I extracted items like lip gloss and coins before throwing them in the washer.) What can I say? I made less than minimum wage. Less meant nothing so I had nothing. The thirty dollars I used to pay for the girls' pizza was all the money I had until I received my father's monthly check which should arrive any day. Which sucked. Which I could pay the rent and my tuition but barely eat.

When I handed them the bakery bag, they didn't

take it. Maya pronounced that dairy was nasal-clogging and the abundance of butter combined with carbohydrate would materialize into fat, and the mucus would quell her windpipes hindering her stellar ability to perform. Thus, no croissant.

"But you play the violin," I said. "You don't need windpipes."

"*No* croissant," she said and held her hand up.

"I'm a vegan," Winona said. "I don't eat animals or anything that comes out of their bodies. Livestock production leads to environmental disaster, deforestation, pollution…"

"Let's just say breeding animals for food is a threat to the planet," Maya interrupted.

"Both of you ate pizza Saturday night," I said. "What about that?"

"It was cheeseless," one of them said.

"With veggies," the other one said.

That evening I received a text message from Maya saying that she needed her royal blue silk blouse for a violin solo she was performing in school at ten on Thursday morning. It had to be dry cleaned. (She must have missed the memo stating what dry cleaning chemicals did to the planet.) I hadn't retrieved the last load of the girls' laundry from the washer yet and when I did I found her blouse. It appeared smaller than I remembered. And crinkly. No problem, I thought. I'd bring it to the twenty-four hour dry cleaners in the morning at eight o'clock after drop off then pick it up at eight Thursday morning on the way home from driving the twins and run it back over to Maya's school. She'd have it before ten. How easy it was to manage teenage girls! You just had to *think*.

That night I poured myself a glass of cheap wine and logged onto Facebook to see what the twins were up to. Maya announced her impending violin performance and bragged how she was chosen for a solo out of twenty-four other students. I drank another glass of wine then another. Winona's status update revealed that her father was still in a coma and her mother remained a pillar of strength and that each night she and her sister read his unconscious being stories from his favorite book by lamplight. The status update reeled in sixty-four heartfelt comments. This propelled me to call Mrs. Yakatori.

"I'm awake," she said. "Mr. Yakatori is still sleeping in a coma."

"That must really suck," I said, half drunk. She agreed. We hung up.

* * *

Day 4 Wednesday

Wednesday confused the hell out of me. This time I had to drop off Maya first, since she had an exam and wanted the extra time to study. Or practice. Or whatever she needed to do. Since we had to leave a half hour earlier, Winona's school did not open their doors until a half hour after we would drop Maya off, therefore, I had to back track. I had to get to the dry cleaners with Maya's blouse before ten so I could collect it before ten the next day in time for her violin solo.

We wove through rush hour traffic in Boston to get Maya to the music academy, then we got stuck in traffic due to construction on the way back to Winona's art school. This is the second time I mixed the twins up.

When we arrived, I gathered Winona's things and waited for her to get out of the car while she applied black lipstick to her lips. She took her books from me but she wouldn't take the violin case. "Don't forget your instrument," I said, pushing it at her.

She stared at me quizzically.

"It's not mine," she said.

"Whose is it?" I said.

"Duh," she said.

Which meant I'd have to drive all the way back to the music academy through traffic and I still had to get to the dry cleaners before ten. I did. Drive back I mean, because Maya would fail her test without her instrument, but I didn't make it to the dry cleaners before ten which meant Maya wouldn't have her blouse for her violin solo.

The music academy took on the grandeur of a palace. It smelled of brass and ointment and students congregated in their coteries here and there speaking in cerebral tones. Now and then notes and chords flowed in the distance. I waltzed through the hallways and found Maya chatting up a colleague outside a classroom. How relieved she'll be when she sees me! And when she saw me I heroically held up the violin case. I was sure to win points in exchange for the screw-up with the silk blouse she'd soon learn about.

"I don't need my violin today," she said, her arms folded across her chest.

"You—you don't?" I said, "but—"

"I told you I have a test," she said, "like, all day."

"Won't you need to play music for your test?"

"It's a written test," she said, "on music theory." She snatched the violin and walked away with her friend.

Boiling over Maya's attitude, I procrastinated on my way to the dry cleaners and arrived at ten-thirty. The woman, Mrs. Chang, ran her business with an iron fist. She told me to come back tomorrow at ten-thirty to pick up the blouse. I supposed rules could be tampered with.

"Can't you make an exception?" I said. "I need it at eight."

"See the sign?" she said. "It says twenty-four hour cleaning, not twenty-two and a half." And that was that. Maya would have to wear a different blouse. I softened and vowed to go through my closet to find something I could lend her. Who was I kidding?

That afternoon my father's check arrived in the mail. I cashed it and bought a Big Mac and a bottle of wine. I poured a full glass and took to Maya's Facebook page as I ate. I noticed that she had a boyfriend named Doug who was older than she and about to graduate from the music academy. Their banter was cute and I felt a particular affection for her until another post read, *Hey sexy bitch, does that porker still drive you to school?* I looked away from my laptop. Porker? Then returned to Maya's reply, *Lol!!! She reeks of ground meat! So gross!* I stopped chewing and put my wine glass down. Winona commented with, *Oooooh that's soooo mean!! She's not that gross.* I logged off and tossed my burger in the garbage and gulped my wine, poured more, and drank until the bottle was gone.

I sent Maya a text message telling her that I forgot to tell her earlier that her blouse wouldn't be ready for her solo. That would fix her, I thought. Teenage girls can be quirky about their clothes—that I knew. She didn't text back.

* * *

Day 5 Thursday

I hated those girls. I kept in mind that when this was over, however it would end, Mrs. Yakatori would reward me. I pulled in the Yakatori's circular driveway the next morning and honked the horn. My eyes were glued to the front door wondering what Maya was going to come out wearing, I mean, what blouse she considered second best to the blue one she could not have. She came sauntering out wearing her royal blue silk blouse. I was dumbstruck. As we drove I looked at her through the rearview mirror. "Maya," I said, "where'd you get your blouse? I mean, how?"

"Neiman Marcus," she said, "but you couldn't afford it."

"I meant that the cleaners wouldn't have it ready until later."

"That was my blouse you took to the cleaners," Winona said.

"Yeah, that was Winona's blouse. My blouse was in my closet the entire time," Maya said, "lucky me."

I wanted out. But Mrs. Yakatori was so goddamned sweet and after all, her husband was fighting for his life. I prayed every night for Mr. Yakatori to snap out of it. Or die. For a split-second I thought that perhaps he'd be better off dead than to deal with girls like this, but I chided myself. Nobody should have to suffer daughters that much to want to die. Besides, it was clear that they loved their father and treated him with respect. Their Facebook pages told me so. I'm sure he was proud of their achievements and loved them too. I saw how he delicately handled the lychee nuts in the supermarket, although he hogged them until I elbowed him in the ribs because he refused to share. He was a gentle man. Selfish, but gentle.

That evening, I had a date. I wore Winona's freshly cleaned royal blue blouse.

The guy's name was Rufus and I met him in a postmodern literature seminar. I wasn't attracted to him, but it was something to do to get my mind off the twins.

Rufus came over and we streamed *The French Lieutenant's Woman* that we had to view for a class. He brought beer and a pizza.

"I don't eat dairy," I said.

"Why not?" he said.

"Dairy's nasal-clogging. It clogs the windpipes," I said. "The abundance of cheese combined with carbohydrates materializes into fat and mucus." I felt so superior. "You should have gotten cheeseless," I said, "with veggies."

"Whatever," he said. "Do you drink beer?"

"Sure." He cracked a beer for me and my mouth watered as I watched him scarf down the hot pepperoni and mushroom pizza.

"I also play the violin," I said. "Did I tell you that?"

Two six packs of Budweiser later I murmured something strange as Rufus slobbered me with kisses and unzipped my jeans. I slurred about having to get up early. Something about having to pick up twins.

* * *

Day 6 Friday

Finally all the twins' laundry was dry, ironed and folded. I stacked the piles neatly back into the canvas laundry bags. I was up since five a.m., hung over, my head pounded and I couldn't sleep. I figured the faster I got things done, the faster I'd be rid of this stint.

A quarter to seven I was about to leave the house to pick up the twins when I noticed something sticking out from underneath the couch. It looked like a crumpled dinner napkin. Was it my underwear? Did it belong to Rufus? How far *did* I go? I realized it had doubled for a dinner napkin in some respect. It was Winona's royal blue silk blouse. No, wait. It was Winona's royal blue silk blouse turned pepperoni pizza stained disgusting shitty not worth crap blouse. Did I eat pizza? I don't remember, as I tripped over an empty bottle of vodka, but Rufus did and I do recall wearing Rufus. In short, I ended up owing Winona three-hundred and seventy-five dollars.

I was ready to rip out my hair. I wanted Mr. Yakatori dead. I called Mrs. Yakatori to end our arrangement and when she answered the first thing she said was, "He squeezed my hand!" This was a good sign, she said, although he was not out of the woods. I couldn't—wouldn't—give up on her now, how could I? She had hope. It would be like Mr. Yakatori squeezing her hand. Then flatlining. I had to stick it out.

* * *

Day 7 Saturday
Finally a day off from chauffeuring the twins—until the phone woke me up at noon. It was Mrs. Yakatori. "Will you take the twins sailing today?" she said. Sailing? What else had I to do? Except finish writing my thesis which I'd been foot-dragging over. I imagined pushing one of the twins in the river.

"Why not?" I said, "I love sailing!" I never sailed in my life. In fact, I hated water and couldn't swim.

My eyes weren't open yet. "Just give me the details," I said through a yawn.

She told me the twins were at the hospital now and since it was a lovely day she suggested a picnic by the Charles River then we'd rent a boat and go sailing. She asked me to come get the girls as soon as I was ready. I had leftover cash from my father's check and remembered to record the cost of the rental.

The twins picked on cucumber rolls and I, seeking to shed my burger chomping reputation, bought a salad at KFC. They drank sparkling water. I drank iced tea from a sippy box. The flavor was a phony lemon. It tasted like cat piss.

After lunch, the twins stretched their ectomorphic bodies on the blanket to catch sunrays. I hoped they had forgotten about sailing.

"I thought we were going sailing," Maya said.

"Don't you need to rent a boat or something, Dora?" Winona said.

Only a quad kayak which held up to four adults was available. The rental cost was twenty-two dollars for one hour, or one-hundred and twenty dollars for the day, minimum one hour. Therefore, I would spend at least twenty-two dollars.

Maze

"Don't you girls have money?" I said, fishing through my wallet.

"We're thirteen," Winona said.

"And we're sad because our father is sick," Maya said.

I wasn't sick but I was mad. I can't even write this scene. Let's just say we went kayaking. Let's say someone fell into the river. Let's say it wasn't Winona and it wasn't Maya who flailed for her life even though she wore a life vest while one of us lit a cigarette that she pulled from behind her ear and watched the bobbing moron. I don't smoke. Neither does Maya.

I refused to log onto Facebook that night for fear I'd strangle one of them. I polished off a bottle of wine and dreamt I lived in a castle that looked like Himeji Castle in Hyogo Prefecture. As I was sitting outside in my garden sipping herbal tea in a balmy breeze something came bellowing out of the sky resembling a two-headed bird-monster and smashed my castle. Some sort of buzzer went off and it wouldn't stop until I answered it.

* * *

Day 8 Sunday

Mr. Yakatori woke up! The nurse phoned me at eight a.m. to deliver the good news. Also, the Yakatoris would like to see me. I stumbled out of bed and threw on shorts and a T-shirt, slipped into flip-flops and was out the door.

When I arrived at the hospital the Yakatori women surrounded a cheerful Mr. Yakatori, who sat up in bed eating tapioca pudding. Mrs. Yakatori sensed my presence and waved for me to enter the room.

"Hi!" I said, "Mr. Yakatori, I'm glad you're well!" Nobody spoke. The sun streamed through the window. It was a glorious day! I handed the car keys to Mrs. Yakatori. She stared at them, then looked at me. I was sure she was going to say that I could keep their car as a reward for taking care of her daughters (at which point I was disappointed that they weren't royalty after all.) I was humbled.

"Gee, Mrs. Yakatori," I said, "I—"

"You want lychee?" she yelled. "You want lychee?"

"I'm sorry?" I said.

"I bet you are," she said.

"*Not*," Maya said.

"Whoa, take it easy," I said.

"You're pathetic," Winona said.

"She flunked art in college, too," Maya said to Winona.

"What kind of moron flunks art?" Winona said.

"W-t-f," I said.

The doctor walked in. He looked like a Ken doll with a stethoscope. "Are you Dora?" he said. I swallowed hard.

"I think so," I said. What were the chances that I could not be Dora today?

"Here," he said. "Fill out these forms please." He handed me a clipboard with a pen attached to it.

"What for?"

"We're billing you," he said, "for Mr. Yakatori's eight day stay. For nearly killing Mr. Yakatori."

"All because of a lychee nut," Mrs. Yakatori said.

"I hope you have money," Winona said, "lots of it."

"I doubt it," Maya said, looking me up and down.

I couldn't believe this was happening. "Your girls are a nightmare!" I snapped at Mrs. Yakatori. I pointed to Mr. Yakatori. "And your husband is a selfish man! And, and—" I couldn't think of what else to say. My brain was a circuit of blown fuses and electric shorts.

"Leave the forms with the nurse, will you?" doctor Ken said, "I've got rounds to make."

"My girls a nightmare?" Mrs. Yakatori said.

"They are not a nightmare, Dora. You are a nightmare." Mr. Yakatori readjusted his glasses that had fallen down his nose and continued merrily tucking into his tapioca.

I took one last look at them.

"I won't pay for anything," I said. "I've paid enough." I threw the keys and the clipboard on the bed.

"Then we sue," Mrs. Yakatori said.

"Then sue," I said, "I've got nothing to lose." And to think I was being sued by foreigners who were better off than I was in my own country.

But that was that. I walked from the dismal medicated hallways of the hospital outside to a gorgeous Sunday afternoon and hopped on a tram to anyplace else (except the supermarket) without the Yakatori sisters. What was it about supermarkets that gave me anxiety? I wrote a story about one man's near death experience because I became ensnared in consumer frenzy in front of a crate of lychee nuts but I couldn't write that man's future and I couldn't at that moment care. My story was not about him, as it would take the spotlight off the Yakatori sisters—heaven forbid.

BROKEN

She carried three shopping bags full of jewelry and expensive clothes in shades of liver and old lace out of the store. Maxing out her credit card would have to be her secret, until the bill came anyway, but what did she forget? The jingling inside her purse confirmed she had her keys. She reached inside and felt her wallet. Her skirt swayed as she fixed herself onto the escalator. Good, she still had on her skirt, but Mnemosyne abandoned her now and the crowded shopping center jarred her nerves. The wisteria walls of the mall gleaned, or winked mysteriously as if in complicity with some twisted force out to engulf her sensibility. An awareness clung to her frame and her aura was a dulled tumbleweed. Her midnight-blue keen-thinking poignant and lucid self seemed to have escaped her. The escalator raced up to the next level. A split-second alarm bell plummeted to her gut—was it the baby? Had she left the baby in the changing room? No, she hadn't taken the baby shopping today. Others began staring at her as she stood stock still. A woman rolled her eyes in disgust. A man gazed at her and shook his head. That was it—it was her head! She had forgotten her head!

Maze

She glided between shoppers up the escalator, took a U-turn at the top of floor K and glided back down the down escalator to floor F and back to the clothing store.

The salesgirl—nineteen, twenty maybe, with jet-black hair and eyes to match, stood affixed to the cash register snapping her gum and tallying up receipts, or something.

"Excuse me," she said to the salesgirl, "have you found a head?"

"Blonde?" the salesgirl said.

"Red," the woman said. "With green eyes," she added, as if.

"Somebody left a blonde head in the fitting room," the salesgirl said. "And her eyes are brown."

"Shit," the woman said. Her voice was all essence. Her senses, too.

"Good luck finding it," the salesgirl shouted through her mouth as the woman left.

She couldn't go home without her head, Bkentz would kill her. Or stick her on the drug. The drug grew a head back between your shoulders, but it wouldn't be the exact old head, it would be a different head with an R tattooed on the forehead to indicate "Replacement." She'd be the laughingstock of society. How embarrassing to throw a dinner party and have your friends, with their original heads intact, suddenly see you've dropped the ball so-to-speak and lost it. It would be the third time she'd lost it, which would elicit expletives from Bkentz, like, "Rebecca, I can't believe you fucked up again. Where was your head?"

The first time Rebecca lost her head she was at a job interview with the promise of a huge salary. A position for salesperson opened up in the want ads and Rebecca secured herself an interview. This was in their pre-baby days and she and Bkentz were saving up for a house. When the interviewer asked Rebecca if she knew how their new product, SuckDust Ceiling Vacuum, functioned (which any idiot could have found information on) she told the truth and said No. Through clenched teeth the interviewer at SuckDust with the austere bun atop her head explained that one simply affixes the apparatus to the ceiling, switches on the light switch and all the dust is sucked to the top in one sweeping rush and how the heck was someone going to sell a product they knew nothing about? Rebecca left the interview chiding herself, "Rebecca," she said, "where was your head?" Surely the woman inside knew that she had no head during the interview. "Always the last to know," Rebecca had murmured to herself, shaking nothing.

The second time she lost her head she was in the car driving with baby Whispt. The baby was cooing in her car seat and surprised Rebecca by uttering the word *banananana*. Rebecca was overwhelmed with joy. All along she thought the baby wasn't developing rapidly enough. She reached into her baby bag, taking her eyes off the road, for a banananana to reward her cooing baby (who had at that instant learned to say the word *banananana*) and swerved into a tree. Thank goodness she was driving at a snail's pace but snails didn't prevent the front end of her car from getting smashed. Snails didn't stop the insurance premium from rising. When she called Bkentz from her cell phone to tell him about Whispt's banananana word and the accident he said, "Damn it, Rebecca! *Where was your head?*"

"I don't know," she responded. "I don't know."

Now this.

Rebecca thought she'd been born with a curse. Born with an uncommon name: Rebecca. How many

Rebeccas did she know? None. How many Rebeccas had she even heard of? Squat. Why couldn't her mother have named her a common name like Bleez or Knmje or Starry-Luz? Rebecca sounds more like a nickname for Rzibka. The salesgirl at the store was named Rzibka, her nametag said so. And what a name! Rzibka or Bleez or Knmje wouldn't have lost *their* heads. People with names like that rarely do. But a Rebecca would. Was her name the problem? What's in a name? A lot, Rebecca thought with her spirit, a lot.

Now, Rebecca lost her head for the third time. Bkentz will hate her for it. Bkentz, the well-bred breadwinner, never lost his. Was she worthy of a man whose mother knew better by choosing a name for her son that made him less susceptible to losing his head? A name that is sure to climb the ranks in the job sector? Bkentz, president and CEO of the company he worked for, managed to execute the responsibilities of his stress-laden job with ease. It baffled Rebecca that Bkentz could be a genius at what he did without breaking a sweat. The long hours at the office. The obscene bonuses at Christmastime rolling in. Bkentzes made money. Bkentzes made sense. Rzibkas made money. Rzibkas didn't lose their heads. She flirted with the idea of hooking Bkentz up with salesgirl Rzibka and running far, far away with baby Whispt. Then she dismissed it. It couldn't be her name, how ridiculous! She was just an airheaded klutz. No wait, she wasn't. She was too self-critical. She had baby brain. Everybody said so. At any rate, she must find her head before Bkentz came home. Bkentz had a dark side she envied.

Rebecca phoned the nanny from the road to dismiss her for the afternoon, saying she was almost home. Rebecca would be ruined if the nanny saw her without her head. She'd snitch. The nanny didn't protest. She was bored anyway, she said. Whispt was asleep in her crib, she said. In her haste Rebecca said goodbye and hung up.

Rebecca was astonished she remembered her phone number. She must be getting better at losing her head. Could it be that the headless were a developed species of their own? What a thought—she could be head of the headless. She'd rename members of the new headless race with archaic names like Mary-Lou and Abe and Johnny. The males would have the male names and the females would have the female names like in the olden days. Not unisex, as it is. She'd tune the world like an instrument. Slow it down. The world, as it was, was too much with us, she thought. Not late but soon.

As she pulled her vehicle onto her street a splinter of euphoria shot through the blueprint of her frame and she prayed the upswing wasn't the better part of her disposition that would plunge into self-destruction. She entered the garage which hadn't been cleaned out in months. Remnants of vacations past—of past Rebecca—tennis rackets and solar-propelled rafts leaned against the walls like dust-caked mummies—were no longer employed for recreation. All this a symbol of the sinkhole that swallowed Rebecca's existence. Her vision was in focus and she wasn't about to crack, what with shards of glumness littering the ground like chunk glass. It was time to turn the switch. Forget Bkentz. Forget baby Whispt. She was on a mission. It would take minutes to wrap up her before life and head out on the road to her after life—and she'd better do it fast for fear what was not visible might soon be lost.

NIPPLE KNOWS BEST

When Hank Nipple woke in his bed one Sunday morning he found himself transformed into a gigantic insect. It was the first BBQ of the season and his wife, Anita, wanted to host a summer-themed costume party for their neighbors. The yard was littered with life-sized flowers and life-sized exotic vacations ambling about and socializing with each other.

Nipple stood at the grill attempting to flip burgers while nursing a Dos Equis.

"Good God," Anita said, flopping over in green flippers worn to resemble petals, "how are you going to flip burgers with those shellfish claws?" She wore a spiky pink wig and Nipple guessed she was dressed up as a tulip, but he'd better not question that for fear he'd a.) Be seen as the idiot he is or b.) Become the butt of Anita's jokes in front of their guests the entire day.

Nipple put on oven mitts and held his hands up. A spatula between them did the trick.

"Do insects even have claws?" his son Aubrey said, moseying over dressed as a band member, which he was.

"No, of course not," his mother mocked. "Where is your band setting up, Aubrey?"

Maybe I should have dressed like a schmuck, Nipple thought to himself. But he knew best. Houseflies have claws. His inspiration for the costume came from *The Fly* which aired the other night on the Syfy channel. But Anita had a point, his claws looked more like lobster claws and if you didn't catch The Fly the other night, well.

"We're performing in the garage," Aubrey said and shrugged.

Anita sighed. "Oh, Aubrey, really? Inside?" She looked up at the overcast sky. "But it's such a beautiful day."

Nipple was assaulted by a neighbor who snuck up from behind in the form of a pineapple palm tree. Nipple high-fived him with his mitt.

"Where's Sam?" the palm asked, too enthusiastically, regarding Nipple's daughter Samantha. Friends joked behind Nipple's back that Samantha had run off to college in sunny California solely to escape the Nipple household in Pittsburgh, as if it were run by fascists, or morons. The subject of Samantha was a sore spot for Nipple. She hardly kept in touch. He suspected she didn't like him much. She had flown in for a short break to catch up with old friends. Nipple hadn't seen her since he picked her up from the airport.

"Sammy had other plans," he said, turning a burger.

"Life's a bitch," the palm tree said. He smacked Nipple on the back and headed for the cooler. The burger slipped from Nipple's grasp and fell through the grid. The screech of an electric guitar screamed through an amp. He took a sip of beer through a straw.

Nipple removed his oven mitt and latched onto the fallen burger with his claw. He brought it back to the surface. "Who's ready for a burger?" he yelled. "I've got one *al dente*," he joked. Nobody laughed. They were too hungry. No wonder people thought he was such a jerk.

It was difficult to be fastidious with claws. Nipple grew tired of being a sucker and suddenly it was Anita's fault. A dark cloud hovered in the distance. Nipple prayed it would make its way to the BBQ and explode over the day like a gray water balloon that had been punctured. Then again, Anita would make him flip burgers in the rain.

"Testing one-two-three, testing one-two-three," rang out of a microphone then Aubrey's band broke into a rendition of the song "Message in a Bottle" by The Police. The band didn't sound half bad. They sounded completely bad. This coming from a man who established his own bad band back in his day.

Flowers and exotic vacations huddled in front of the open garage door clutching bottles of beer. The rain cloud inched toward the Nipple residence at a snail's pace. Nipple was desperate for a storm. Even if it meant getting his mitts wet.

A year has passed since I wrote my note… came banging out of the lead singer's mouth.

A tap on the shoulder brought Nipple hope. He was hankering for conversation. Or maybe hankering to complain about costume parties.

A straw hut stood with an unopened beer. "Hey Nipple, could you lend me a hand?"

Nipple removed a mitt and his claw transformed into a bottle opener. At least he was good for something. The hut took a sip through a door of a mouth and headed toward the garage. The hut's roof turned around, held up the bottle and said, "Thanks a lot."

"Isn't Aubrey's band amazing!" Anita said, totally cocked. 'Amazing' was her favorite word. "Come support him," she said, taking Nipple by his hairy fly arm. He wore a black ski mask over his head and two ping pong balls were pasted where his eyebrows were to mimic bug eyes.

"In a minute. The burgers are almost ready."

Nipple was adamant about getting the food perfect, not because he wanted his friends to enjoy it, he did, but he'd rather prove that he could grill good burgers dressed as a gigantic fly.

"It'll take a second. Let Aubrey see that you're interested," Anita persisted.

The band was on a role. *Sending out another text … Sending out another text… Sending out another text…*

Sandwiched between a marigold and a cruise ship, Nipple hung loose and started to enjoy himself. He thought Aubrey's band put a good contemporary spin on the lyrics. He bobbed his head to the beat and he tapped his foot. Then the marigold leaned into him and said, "Nipple is a drip, don't you think? I came here today because I didn't feel like cooking and my husband wanted free beer."

The smell of burnt meat came from the direction of the grill. Smoke billowed over and filled everyone's nostrils. The guests swung their heads toward their sullied lunch. The smoke moved in sync with the approaching rain cloud. The cloud glided faster and faster, until it stopped right above Nipple, marking the spot.

"Where's Nipple?" somebody said.

He raised his arms above his head and braced himself for the inevitable downpour.

SMOKING

The thrilling part about starting to smoke is that everyone around me is trying to quit. Choosing a brand of cigarette is personal, like a political standpoint or a social stance. I settle on Camel because the packaging is neat. I love animals. But the choices are maddening: filtered, unfiltered, menthol, crush, lights, wides, 99s, whatever. It's like choosing a topping for your pizza at lunch. Which, thank goodness for cigarettes, I will no longer eat.

I head down to the elementary school playground and hide behind a brick building (the gym where I used to suck at dodge ball) to drag on my first cigarette. While inside children are learning how to divide and conquer, I'm fourteen and a virgin all over again, except this time, I'm not a goody-goody bible thumping nerd who is afraid to toke. I smoke. I shiver because it's winter and I'm in a black leather jacket wearing black knit gloves with the fingers cut out. I smoke Camel unfiltered because, I thought, if I'm going to smoke, I'm going *to smoke*. I take a drag and suddenly there's a slew of motorcycles pulling up inside my lungs. All noise and smog.

My pleural cavity is pierced by exhaust. Ouch, the burning pipes. I take another puff and another and I hop on my own Harley, grabbing the handlebars by the horns. I'm revving up. I never look back. I'm a siren in a black and white photograph. I'm New York City. I'm San Francisco. I'm Allison Glee who was cool in seventh grade.

I am no longer bored, because *Life, friends, is boring* or life became boring. But not if you smoke. Boredom is suspended for approximately five minutes (unless you chain smoke, which I will learn by the end of my habit can be an expensive habit, that you could rack up cigarettes like the minutes on a long distance phone call.) You never have to leave the minutes as long as you are smoking. I've concluded that smoking is healthy if only because I am a smoker now.

I'm addicted to my new addiction and suddenly it's Sunday. I was never so happy with ennui. I drive to the mall. I ask for a soft pack of Camel unfiltered at the kiosk and the man with a zillion tattoos tells me he only has the filtered ones in hard pack and gives me a scrunched up look like he's about to cry but actually he's imitating my expression. He turns around to get the filtered ones. I give his back the finger.

I'm sitting on a bench observing obesity saunter in and out of stores. Shoppers tug at sweatshop-inspired clothing hanging on metal racks. Some loiter while finishing triple scoop ice cream cones, the air is redolent with oregano and suddenly I crave pizza. My hard pack of tobacco gems is waiting in my coat pocket. My attention turns to the escalator delivering hoards of people with mounds of shopping bags: teenagers with jeans slung below their waists, whining toddlers fidgeting in their strollers, bickering couples. All of them step off to the barely audible pulse of Muzak and slink away in all directions. I'm thinking, one of these people could very well open fire and shoot up the mall. I'm hoping it will be today. I'm feeling suicidal. I whip out a cigarette and light up: anxiety is squelched. I puff and puff and puff. I'm floating with the Muzak. I am no longer hungry. I'm happy to be thin. I'll pick on a bowl of pasta later, but for now I'm skinny and I'm happy smoking up a hard pack of Camel filtered cigarettes (because the man at the crappy kiosk didn't have Camel unfiltered cigarettes) on a steel bench in a crowded mall on a Sunday with nothing else better to do. I go to the Ladies Room. It stinks of saccharine cherry-scented toilet cleaner. As I pull down my jeans my cell phone falls out of my back pocket and into the toilet. At least it wasn't my hard pack.

Stephanie, my teenaged daughter, is waiting, arms folded, for me at the garage door when I get home.

"Where were you?" she says, tapping her foot. "You're late."

"I was at the mall," I say, holding up a shopping bag.

"What's that smell?" she says.

"What smell?" I say. "I don't smell a smell."

"I don't know," she says, "it smells like—the public. Were you—*smoking?*"

"The public?" I say. "Smoking?" I say.

"Hypocrite," she says.

I brush past her and she follows me. "You were supposed to be home an hour ago," she says. "The kitchen's a mess and I'm supposed to cook dinner tonight and how am I supposed to cook dinner when the kitchen's a mess?"

"So clean it," I say.

"It's not my mess," she says, "it's your ugly mess."

"Watch your mouth."

"What did I say?"

"That my life is an ugly mess. Go out and shovel the snow in the driveway for a consequence."

"I shoveled it," she says.

"Then shovel the front walk," I say.

"The boy down the block did it for thirty bucks," she says.

"Shovel the lawn then."

I sneak into the bathroom. I need one badly. I vowed never to smoke when the family was at home but I must. Stephanie is on my back and I have an ugly mess of dishes to load. When did this all start? This loss of control? I sit on the toilet, lid down, window open, incense lit, and take drag after drag after drag. When I come out I run into my bedroom and try on my new red boots. Stephanie comes in. I'm turning all around in front of the mirror admiring my new cool high-heeled boots that I'm going to wear when I start going to new cool clubs with my new blonde hair and my manicured nails which is the future version of myself that is forever fixed inside my head. I never materialize.

"Those boots are hideous," Stephanie says. "You're too old for them."

"Don't say that."

"Why?"

"Because it isn't nice."

"Dinner's ready," she says. "I cleaned your mess. And dad called. He'll be home late again. He tried calling you, where's your cell phone?"

"I don't have a cell phone."

The front door opens and my son walks in from hockey practice.

"What's for dinner?" he says.

"Pasta Pesto," Stephanie says.

"You bitch," he says and he slaps her face. This means he approves. This is how the family communicates. This is how we use speech.

Later on I slip into bed with my not-yet-new not-yet-sexy lingerie that remains decked on the woman in my head but I don't wait. When my husband says he is coming home late, *it will be late*. I turn on the TV. I light up. I no longer care about getting caught. Smoking is my whirlwind romance and I remind myself of the dangers youthful habits create. What if I fall asleep and burn the house down? I am thrilled. But sometimes, I remind myself not to think about it too much. That sometimes a cigarette is just a cigarette.

BLIND DATE

I enter Rusty's Place on the lower east side and claim my usual table in the back. I'm reluctant to meet the stranger I met online in a bar, especially a girl like me who hasn't dated anyone since my traveling circus days, but my confidence is soaring and I don't know why. You wouldn't know why either if you saw me.

I light a cigarette. My doctor says I should quit smoking but I can't. Rusty's Place is the only public spot I'm comfortable in because people don't stare at me and Rusty is a gem.

I'm about to chicken out but I have an obligation to fulfill. Rusty comes over and offers me gin. I shoo him away, I say, "I'm waiting for someone, don't cramp my style. Just give me peanuts."

He acts surprised. "You're meeting a—guy?"

"Not just any guy," I say. "Snarky2000." Smoke rings happen. "He's got black hair like shoestring licorice," I say.

I tell Rusty I met Snarky2000 online and we've chatted for months. I tell Rusty that I love Snarky2000. I love him so much even though I never met him. That every time he comes online my heart goes *ping*. "I'm in love with a screen name," I say. "I'm in love with the concept of online dating tucked inside that little black font." As if this quells any fear about meeting someone in the flesh. In a bar. Besides, I'm not technically meeting him *in* a bar, I'm meeting him *at* a bar. "There's a difference," I say.

"Whatever you say," Rusty says.

I've been searching for love forever. I am desperate for companionship. But whenever a man gets too close, he runs away.

Snarky2000 doesn't know what I look like. "No photo," he'd said. He was satisfied with just my phone number because he got off on my voice and mine was a sweet one. He thinks I'm two-hundred and thirty pounds thinner than I am. What he doesn't know is that I'm a three-hundred and sixty pound knockout. I told him I am an office assistant. I didn't tell him I applied for a job as an exotic dancer at Rusty's because I didn't get hired. I asked Rusty if my busting the pole out of the ground had any bearing on his decision. "Maybe I swing too low? Too slow?"

"Too fat, kid," he'd said.

The door at Rusty's swings open dramatically, ushering in a breeze. The Happy Hour crowd shuffles in. I down three bowls of peanuts.

A shadow cuts a figure in the light. It's him. He orders a beer and asks Rusty something I can't hear. Rusty winks and nods in my direction. Snarky eyes the joint, but skims past me. My table in the corner smolders in a soft gray haze. Pinball machine bells go *bling* and *bling*. Rusty leans over and whispers in Snarky2000's ear. Snarky2000 searches the room, his eyes skip over me—then back again. He picks up his drink. He's headed my way.

As he steps closer into the light, I see his hair, black and swept back over his head, greasy and stiff. He's got a decent build. He's wearing dark glasses. He's holding a cane.

"Are you Nanette?" he says to the air.

I shrug.

"Speak," he says.

I open my mouth and swallow a fourth refill of peanuts. The vibes I get say Snarky's on the level, but in the dark recesses of reality, my comfort zone is shattered by self-doubt. I grab my purse. Wedged in tight, I suck in my breath and attempt to maneuver myself out from between the table and the bench, in what I can only describe as the beginning of a stampede, and manage to take the whole table with me.

"Where're you going?" Rusty asks as I blow by him.

But I don't answer. I'm already out the door.

PRELUDE TO THE AFTERNOON OF A FAUN

I returned downstairs to the living room to find four-year-old Charlotte standing in front of the open face of a humungous dollhouse, a foot taller than herself, with her head peering inside an upstairs bedroom. Her father, Jean Pierre, was fast asleep on the living room couch. We had just driven ten hours, counting stoppage time for Charlotte, from Montreux, Switzerland, to his holiday house in the south of France and everyone was exhausted. Debussy's "Prelude to the Afternoon of a Faun" was playing on Jean Pierre's old record player. This was Charlotte's favorite composition, its haunting melody was part of the atmosphere in which she thrived. During the car ride, she bounced up and down in her seat, "*Prélude à l'après-midi d'un faune! Prélude à l'après-midi d'un faune!*" I desperately needed a drink. I plucked a Bordeaux off the wine rack. Jean Pierre rolled over and continued slumbering as deeply as I left my mother upstairs in the guest bed. Charlotte gave me a terrified look.

"Where's Sylvia?" she asked.

"Don't worry, Charlotte, she's sleeping." I

popped the cork. "She nodded off about ten minutes ago and I think she'll sleep into the night."

She turned back around and said, "*Sylvia est une sorcière!*" In her hand was a six-inch piece of pink yarn.

"What's the yarn for?" I said.

She looked at the yarn, as if she forgot she was holding it. Then she furrowed her brow and said, as if I were stupid, "It's for a *noose*." She turned back to the dollhouse. "Cindy is going to hang herself."

"Who is Cindy?" I asked.

"Lilly's sister."

"Who is Lilly?"

"Kristina's daughter."

"Who is Kristina?"

She gave me a condescending glance. "The mother of Cindy and Lilly," she said.

I forgot why I cared who these dolls were so I shut up and poured myself a glass of wine. I stumbled over to the couch and sat at the end by Jean Pierre's feet and tucked my legs underneath myself. Charlotte dropped the yarn and went over to the bathroom where she washed her hands with hot water and soap. She remained scrubbing at the sink for five minutes. She did this almost every fifteen or twenty minutes and by nightfall she will have washed her hands approximately fifty times.

"Isabel, could you help me tie the noose?" she said when she returned.

"Sure," I said. "Give it to me." I placed my wine on the coffee table. Charlotte handed me the yarn and sat on the floor watching as I carefully constructed a small knot and—*voila!*—the noose was complete. She swiped strands of hair from her face in one quick jerk and gently took the noose. "*Merci.*"

At that moment I wished she were my child. I was fascinated by her beauty, which was quite ugly, I could have observed her forever. She had prominent features that didn't fit her face. Hair parted on the side, it fell in dirty blond waves to her shoulders. Sand-colored face with freckles, deep brown eyes that could stop any sea from rolling. She looked familiar to no one. I wondered what Jean Pierre's late wife looked like. As for me. Well. You could use your imagination. I looked familiar to everyone.

The words *"Prélude"*—*"à l'après-midi"*—*"d'un faune!"* still chanted in my head.

Charlotte took one of her dolls, a Barbie doll, and

put the noose around its neck. She stood in front of the dollhouse searching for a place to hang her. She poked her head into each room then stood back. She was perplexed. I could have suggested objects, like the dining room chandelier, or the tiny plant hanger that jutted out from the side of the dollhouse, but I thought it best that the little girl's creative process develop on its own. She turned to me, frustrated. Then turned back and studied each room. I opened my mouth but it was her voice that happened: "The chandelier."

"Good choice, Charlotte." I took a sip of wine. She attempted to tie a knot around the metal neck of the chandelier with fierce concentration, but the noose kept slipping off the doll's head.

"It's too big," she said. "The loop is too big."

As I examined the intensity on her face, I asked, "Why does Cindy want to die?" She ignored me.

"There," she said. She taped the loop to the Barbie doll's neck and taped it all to the dollhouse's kitchen wall. Barbie was standing. Her feet touched the ground.

"Cindy is dead," she announced proudly.

"Not dead," I said. I swallowed my wine in one

gulp. "Cindy's still standing." I poured another glass. "What you could do, Charlotte, is bend her legs at the knees. This way she won't touch the floor." Charlotte examined the situation with careful precision. She cocked her head one way. Then the other.

"Her knees don't bend," she said.

I hadn't noticed. Did Ken's knees bend? I wondered. "Do Ken's knees bend?" I asked.

"Who's Ken?" she said.

"Never mind." I glanced out the picture window. The rain stopped and a rainbow spread herself over the Mediterranean like a woman in heat.

"Hey, Charlotte, I know," I was about to score points with my new lover's wunderkind, "since Cindy is in the kitchen, why not stick her head in the oven? She could gas herself instead." She gave me an expression that told me, once again, I was stupid. "It's electric," she said in a you-don't-know-shit tone that made me want to slap her.

"What?"

"The oven," she said. "The oven is electric. Not gas."

"It's a toy, Charlotte. It could be anything you want it to be."

She smirked. As I was about to suggest that the doll swallow an overdose of pills, I remembered that the doll's mouth was painted over in plastic and spared myself the humiliation of a new label. I lit a cigarette and wondered if Jean Pierre kept a gun in the house. Charlotte rose to her ritual.

Charlotte was the most fucked up four-year-old I ever met. Jean Pierre had told me that she was obsessed by death. She didn't want friends. She was smitten with suicide and anyone who committed it. She ate nothing but vegetables and coffee. What is Charlotte but for a character in a story? If I were to write a review on Charlotte, it might look like this: "An exhilarating ride through childhood. A Psychological thriller."—*Isabel X, Charlotte's father's latest lover.*

Meanwhile, *Prelude* rolled softly in the background.

End flute. Enter oboe.

Charlotte wanted to be an artist and paint for a living just like her father when she grew up. She reveled in a new artist each month. This month it was van Gogh. Jean Pierre read to her from a book about his life, she knew everything there was to know about him and could identify most of his work. Expressionism was a relief, as last summer Charlotte was a Dadaist and blasted again and again a hideous recording she copped off the internet.

She sat on my lap and flung her arms around my neck, holding her stuffed rabbit, who had half its left ear lobbed off. She smelled of violet soap. "Let's go upstairs and spy on Sylvia," she whispered. Her father was out cold and didn't stir. It was going to be one hell of a week, I thought.

Back again to flute.

"Not a good idea," I said.

"Why not?" she said.

"Because Sylvia hasn't been well, Charlotte. She needs to rest, this is why we took her here." I thought this was a good opportunity to bond with the girl. "You see, Charlotte…" But she shot off my lap and was halfway up the stairs before I finished my sentence. I chased after her, shouting softly, "Charlotte, *stop!* Charlotte, *don't! Charlotte—!*" Sylvia thinks my brother Trey hanged himself a year ago. Sylvia hadn't been mentally stable since. But how could I expect Charlotte to sympathize with that? On the car ride over, Charlotte insisted they play hangman in the backseat, where they sat side by side, to pass the time. Charlotte wins no trophy for tact, at the same time she cannot be accused of insensitivity, not because of her age, but because this precocious sea vegetable never met my brother. As it was, Sylvia went wild with rage at Charlotte's suggestion. Spitting and shouting. She told the child exactly why she wouldn't play and now Charlotte thought Sylvia was going to hang her, too.

Charlotte was quick and she was waiting for me at the guest room door, her hand on the knob. She wanted to catch Sylvia in the midst of the ultimate form of human vulnerability: sleep. She gave me a sinister smile.

"Go ahead, Charlotte. See what Sylvia has to say." I stood, arms akimbo, and challenged her.

"If Sylvia is the noise I want to hear," she said.

"What Sylvia isn't," I said, "is the piece spinning calm on the turntable downstairs. So let's go." I headed down the stairs certain that she was trailing behind me. I went over to the couch and poured more wine. I sat a moment or two, savoring the music. Charlotte wasn't with me. I went back up. She was still standing with her hand on the knob. I lit another cigarette. As smoke flowed from my mouth I said, "I thought you were afraid of her, Charlotte."

"Why should I be afraid of an old woman?" she said.

"Because you talk too much."

She peeped through the keyhole. "She looks dusty," she said.

"Let me see." I pushed her out of the way. There was Sylvia, recumbent on the mattress, still as water and just as deep. A grey hue shrouded her and hung independently from the lingering lamplight that cast a yellow tinge in the room from a corner we couldn't see. I had given her a tranquilizer when we arrived, what with her outburst in the car.

Charlotte, her back against the wall, slid down slowly and took a seat on the hallway floor. She looked distressed.

Large raindrops splashed, widely dispersed, on the skylights. I sat down on the floor next to her and lit up again.

"How will Cindy die?" she said.

Drop, drop, drop.

"She won't," I said, staring straight ahead at a burgundy painted wall, flicking cigarette ashes on the floor.

"Why not?" she said.

"Because she's dumb." I took a long drag. "Only intellects—really smart people—commit suicide, Charlotte."

"Why?" she said.

"Because they live in a world that's too small for them."

"So, if I'm an intellect, will I commit suicide?"

"Ambitious, aren't you?—but no. Not all intellects commit suicide. Only most people who commit suicide happen to be intellectual."

She considered this.

Downstairs the music stopped. "The music stopped," I said. "Shall I replay the record?"

"No," she said, "it replays itself, haven't you been listening?"

Un. Deux. Trois.

The melody began and Charlotte was lost in its maze of musical cells. A harmonic fluidity that conducted her world. I was lost in the maze of Charlotte. I grew fond of her fast. Charlotte wasn't ill. I'd miswritten her. Charlotte's behavior was the repercussion of a grandiose instance.

A series of clouds moved in on the eight p.m. sun.

Prélude à l'après-midi d'un faune.

The record played over again and over again. My head rested on my shoulder and the next thing I knew I woke to a smell that I can only describe as wicked. My cigarette had been smoldering and cast a black hole in the carpet. Charlotte hadn't noticed. Charlotte wasn't there. Or maybe I was someplace else. I heard running water. Charlotte was back.

"Charlotte, how long have I been asleep?"

She shrugged her shoulders. "I don't know."

"Tell me this then. How many times have you washed your hands since I'd been asleep?"

"I don't know."

I calculated that she must have washed her hands more than once, or she would have known. Therefore, I'd been sleeping for at least thirty minutes.

"But you've slept through five Preludes," she said. This was how Charlotte measured time.

"Are you hungry?" I knew she'd decline but it was my nurturing instinct to ask anyway. "Would you like me to heat up the duck cassoulet we took home from the restaurant?"

"I don't like meat," she said. "*Je voudrais une tasse de café.*" She sat back down. I could tell she was tired.

I made her instant coffee with no milk, no sugar, while her mind swam in the music that told her she was significant. Our luggage was splayed by the front door. I gathered Charlotte's nightgown and toothbrush. We'd unpack the rest in the morning.

"Here you go." She was about to take a sip of coffee. Then, with a sudden bolt of energy, she sprang up, having forgotten my mother and peered through the keyhole.

"She's still there," she said.

"I know," I said. I was tired, too.

"Come, Charlotte. It's getting late." I handed her her nightgown and took her by the hand.

"I'm too tired to sleep," she said. Charlotte, I might add, does not know how to sleep. She is a die-hard insomniac. What I mean is, she falls asleep, but she does not stay asleep.

To step into Charlotte's room was to strike strange. A merriment of colors exploded about the room's expand. Stimulating yet depressing. The walls were painted in shocking pink with lemon yellow molding. A poster of *Das Kotsbild* hung over her bed from her Dada days. Wall to wall carpet, a field of peridot. A throw rug in midnight blue. Tubes of pastels were strewn about. Caps missing, paint oozing. Watercolors. Oils. A half-emptied jar of linseed oil. Oiled cloth. Piles of books askew in one corner, from the works of Cézanne to Warhol. Rimbaud, Goethe, Shakespeare, Donne.

Prélude à l'après-midi d'un faune!

She changed into her white nightgown with yellow flowers on it and moved to the bathroom to exercise her ritual one last time before bed. I tiptoed downstairs, past the couch that cradled Jean Pierre for the night, and gathered the turntable and record. When I returned, Charlotte was tucked into her four-poster bed. I set up the turntable and its speakers on a small table meant to entertain elegant dolls with tea parties that would never be. I carefully placed the needle on the album.

"Did you brush your teeth?"

"*Oui.*"

A flute solo intruded whatever it was I was to say next and I sat on the edge of the bed savoring the passage with her. My attention was drawn to an easel in one corner of the room with a half painted canvas, upstrokes feverishly wincing, light blue and violet oils. A swirl of green. A smear of orange. It might have been a wheat field. It might have been the sea.

"What were you painting?" I said. She looked confused. Or maybe she was concentrating.

"It's finished," she said.

"What's finished?"

She turned her head in the painting's direction, but she didn't focus on it. Her eyes were fixed on nothing. "The painting," she said. "It's finished."

I followed her gaze slowly, my eyes from her eyes and focused on nothing with her.

The rain fell in sheets, drowning out the flute.

"What is it?" I asked her, staring in the same direction as she.

"My mother's death," she said.

I turned to her. "The painting?"

"*Oui.*"

"Do you want to talk about it?" I said.

"No," she said, "I just want to look at it." Her eyes moved up toward the canvas and rested there.

"No, I meant your mother. What happened to your mother?"

"She died," she said. She rolled over and shut her eyes. "Daddy and I went to the beach one day last summer."

"What happened at the beach?"

"Nothing. My mother stayed home and when we got back she was dead."

Enter oboe.

"Had she been sick?" I said.

"No," she said. "She had been sad."

I didn't press her. If she wanted to talk, she would talk.

The rain tapered off and I cracked a window to let the metallic scent in.

"Charlotte? Can I read you a story?" She reached over, not opening her eyes and grabbed a book off her nightstand and handed it to the air. While other children her age around the world were listening to their parents read Dr. Seuss, she opted for Keats. The sound of waves hit the shore in the distance.

Darkling, I listen.

And back to flute. Clarinet.

…and, for many a time/I have been half in love with easeful death.

Violas. Violins. I read:

"'My heart aches, and a drowsy numbness pains/ My sense, as though of hemlock I had drunk,/Or emptied some dull opiate to the drains…'"

Maze

Charlotte's breathing became deep, in sync with the melody. As sleep closed in on her, the melody was exhausting itself to its end.

Past the near meadows, over the still stream,/Up the hill-side; and now 'tis buried deep/In the next valley-glades: Was it a vision, or a waking dream?/ Fled is that music:—Do I wake or sleep?

ISABEL B.

Isabel B. was simply exquisite. While reading Boccaccio's interpretation of Helen in *Famous Women*, I pictured only Isabel. Not just the physical attributes, but the grandeur of his analysis. To describe Isabel's beauty is the antithesis of Boccaccio's account of Helen: where Helen's bright eyes were full of happiness, Isabel's eyes were saturated in sorrow. Where he depicted the pleasant serenity of Helen's entire face and her charming changes of expression, Isabel's was profoundly unemotional. I saw a mysterious woman pained by something I could never understand. A dreamer, I felt compelled to help her, become the chivalrous knight women in fiction waited for. I never initiated a romantic relationship with any of my students, but that made no difference. She didn't behave like the typical smitten schoolgirl—Isabel wasn't interested. I couldn't even fantasize about her. Every time I created a scenario in my mind with the two of us together, her eyes undoubtedly fastened onto my reverie.

It was my last semester teaching English literature at a university in northern Italy. Three times a week for three months Isabel sat in the back of my class without uttering a word. She never raised her hand to speak, and I never called on her. She exceeded most of the students in age by ten years, she was thirty-two, nine years younger than me. She was the only native speaker of English and I felt my words fall into the clutches of her scrutiny. I turned on the most intellectual English vocabulary I knew. Was my pronunciation correct? Was I fluent enough to convey the lesson to the class? I glanced her way for clues. I'd even try to impress her with a rhetoric full of Americanisms. Her gaze never shifted from the notebook on her desk. I didn't understand why I was desperate for her approval until it hit me—I, the guy voted by his colleagues least likely to commit to one woman and get married, was in love. Soon I discovered wherever love goes, his evil twin misery follows.

One morning, elated over my awakening, I noticed the diamond wedding band on her left ring finger and had to face the ugly truth. Hoping I was mistaken, I rummaged through her file in the admissions office and found her application to the university with a summary about herself and why she had come abroad. She was a poet. Apparently she had lived in many cities before settling here. Her husband was a financial genius who made an obscene income. I was familiar with where she lived. It was a wealthy area in the hills. Did her husband travel often for business? Was she lonely? A woman accustomed to a lifestyle with a rich man would never think twice about me. What with the modest salary I shoved into my savings each month, what did I have to offer? If I trashed all my lectures and instead professed my unremitting attraction to her, would she give up her six, or seven-room house, which was indicative to the area in which she lived, for my two-room flat? Besides, we had nothing in common. She was a poet in the twenty-first century marching ahead, and I, fixed in literature of the past. Would she be willing to meet in the middle?

After a long day of grading research papers in my cramped office I went home. I saved Isabel's paper for last. I wanted to be as comfortable as possible and couldn't wait to delve into it. Reading her paper will be the key, I thought, since I couldn't obtain any of her poetry anywhere, to see what makes her tick. She had written it on the evolution of language in verse from Old English to the present. At first, egocentrically, I thought she was reaching for me by compromising our contrasting loves of literature, then concluded she had chosen a topic of interest solely for herself as a poet. I took my time. I poured myself a glass of wine, lit a cigarette and traded my beloved Puccini for Wagner (I was in a mood) and set it thrashing in the background. I scanned the table of contents. It was flawless. Her introduction was polished and concise. Succinctness mattered to me, although I wasn't sure if my assessment at that point was accurate or if I was biased. As I read further, I froze. Was she mocking me? The rest of her paper was written entirely in iambic pentameter with open couplets. I was certain I explained to my class the guidelines for writing a research paper. Why didn't she pay attention? Easygoing as I was, nothing a student ever said or did in my career as a professor peeved me until now. Isabel! The pace of my heart accelerated, I knew I'd have to meet with her in my office to discuss it. I couldn't accept her paper the way it was written, and I surely couldn't fail her. She'd have to rewrite it the right way. In private we'd sit and I'd offer her my undivided attention. Something would have to click between us. I'd make her love me too.

I fidgeted at the keyboard of my computer to write her an e-mail. First: "Dear Isabel, I perused your research paper with glee and found it stimulating. Unfortunately, a minor problem has surfaced. Please visit my office at your earliest convenience so we may examine it together." No way. Then: "Dear Isabel, Your paper was absolutely insightful. Although I enjoyed it more than the others, I regret that you must rewrite it. If you stop by my office at your earliest convenience, I would be more than happy to take the time and go over it with you." What mawkish idiot had love reduced me to? Finally: "Dear Ms. B, There is a problem concerning your paper. You need to see me during my office hours." That was that. I checked the message in the "mail sent" folder several times that evening to make sure I didn't inadvertently sign my name, "Love, Professor X—"

She wore a frumpy floral print dress fit for an old lady. The color was unflattering against her artificially tanned skin and it hid her ballerina-perfect figure. I didn't remember her being so round. She wasn't beautiful up close. Her eyes were close together and beady, caked with make-up—blue clumping mascara and a sparkling rose-colored eye shadow. Her lips imitated thick wax in an orange-red lipstick. I don't usually notice this kind of detail on a woman, but the tackiness of this cheap rip-off of the goddess I knew was pronounced.

When she looked at me she was glowing. It was the first time I ever saw her smile and that moment I knew she returned my feelings. I scoffed in the face of unrequited love. The look of sorrow I longed for had vanished from her entirely and she was transformed into a giddy schoolgirl. She hung on my every criticism, nodding her head while batting her eyelashes frantically. She repeated how sorry she was that the paper was stupidly written. Where did her supreme demeanor go? I was no longer interested. My phone rang and I was relieved it would bring an abrupt end to our meeting. But the phone rang incessantly, even after I picked up the receiver. Isabel must have left. When I looked up, I was alone in a dark cold room. In a dark cold bed. It was morning.

My office hours came and suddenly I had nothing to do. Except of course sit and wait for Isabel. I reflected briefly on my dream. Isabel hadn't replied to my e-mail so I didn't know what time (or if) she'd arrive. I was hoping she'd come last, so we wouldn't be rushed. I'd be distracted if I knew students conjugated outside my office waiting to see me.

She came first. When she entered my office I was floored. It was the first time I looked into her eyes and noticed they were pale green. They were so light they looked almost invisible against a backdrop of olive skin. Naturally beautiful, she hadn't a trace of make-up on. Sable curls cascaded past her shoulders to the middle of her back. Her figure was stunning. Above all, she didn't deviate from the superior air that possessed her. I sensed her impatience and that I was wasting her time. Her aura grabbed hold of my insides and twisted them into knots. I couldn't speak. She spoke first, confidently defending her paper. She covered all angles of her research. She spoke rapidly and I loved the way her eyes blinked at the start of each sentence. I managed to tell her it was only an issue of form and handed her *A Manual for Research Papers in English Literature.* She looked at it for a minute and rolled her eyes. Then the almond-shaped green of them fell upon Boccaccio's

Famous Women that sat on my desk. Convinced that our *tête-à-tête* would take a tactical turn, I asked her if she read it. This would leave the door wide open for conversation. The version I owned was written in Latin and Italian and she said, "Very funny," and left my office. Her perfume lingered in the air.

But dreams also take place in daytime. They are called daydreams. So alone I sat, waiting. Then a single knock came, but it was student X then Y then Z rolling in one after the other and suddenly, there went the morning. Isabel never showed up.

I had predicated who the last student to visit me would be and became apprehensive. It was Katrina H. Katrina had been flirtatious the entire semester and I never thought about getting involved with her, but ego-raped over my non-existent meeting with Isabel, Katrina would have to be the drug to mask the ache. I knew she'd be easy. A teacher could tell. Each semester there would be one in class who was an open book. The one who'd sit in the front row with the alluring look in her eye, asserting that she was interested beyond the text. The one who would repeatedly visit your office even when it wasn't your office hours and chat about topics unrelated to class.

I was not exactly innocent. Of course I wanted my students to excel, so when I reciprocated mildly to flirtations, they'd respond by striving harder. Katrina was the classic example, although at times her persistence was more obvious than most. She would stay after class every day to ask unnecessary questions. She'd be the last to visit during my office hours and stay long. Often she'd bring me little surprises, a cappuccino, wild flowers, or, what I favored most, copies of literary journals containing Italian translations. She'd sit close to me and lavish me with compliments. I'd posit myself as far back as possible from her and act friendly but serious, and patiently wait for her to finish talking. I didn't want to discourage a student in any way. But I didn't want to lead one on either.

My head still spun with Isabel. I craved her. And just as I decided to pull her aside after class one day, she was gone. Then she kept on being gone.

Katrina was the quintessential blonde, blue-eyed girl. I grew used to her visits. I grew used to *her*. She was intellectual, well-spoken, and offered keen insight into our discussions. As a matter of fact, she was the top student in my class. I started seeing her and we were together until the semester ended. We had sex constantly. Everywhere. But each time I was with Katrina, I was lonelier for Isabel. What was she doing each moment? Writing a poem? Making love to her husband? I imagined what it must be like in bed with her. Her husband must have made love to her every night. I would have. When I spent time with Katrina I pictured Isabel with every emotion that Katrina projected. Would Isabel have reacted angrily to the same situation? What would Isabel's opinion have been? Would *this*, or *that*, make Isabel laugh?

I knew Isabel wouldn't drop out, she was graduating in June that year. My days with her were numbered and I had to reach her somehow. One thing I never discussed with Katrina was another student, but I was dying to ask her if she had anything on Isabel. Katrina was intuitive and I trusted she would give me an accurate assessment. Our affair died off, but we remained friends. So I took a chance and asked if she knew her. "Isabel?" she said. "The redhead who sits in the front?" "Actually," I told her, "no. The raven haired goddess who sat in the back." All right, so I worded it slightly different, but she told me that she had heard from a medical student, who had an internship at the university hospital, that a woman, perhaps her name was Isabel, or Iris, or something with an "I", had a nervous breakdown and almost drowned. It was speculative whether or not she tried to commit suicide, but Katrina discounted it. She heard this woman was happy and led a privileged life.

"Perhaps it was a rumor," Katrina concluded, "and she is probably fine." Probably. But I wanted to know for sure. Sensing that it wasn't a good idea to press her further, I let Katrina continue. She heard from her friend that this woman was a foreigner, and had a family in Spokane. She may have moved back there.

"Didn't she have a husband?" I asked.

Katrina threw me an impish look. "Husband? I'm not sure, why? Why are you so interested in her?"

I dropped the subject. I believed Katrina had Isabel confused with somebody else.

It was summer and I'd be moving on as visiting professor at another university south. Instead of enjoying my break, I tortured myself over Isabel. I envisioned her on the brink of insanity and imagined

I was the one who rescued her from her fate with my confessions of longing and love. I drove myself crazy looking for her and was thwarted by unlisted phone numbers, invalid e-mail addresses and a wrong home address. There was no Isabel B. listed in Spokane either. I searched the internet, I made telephone calls. I exhausted myself for months searching all ends of the earth for her. Nobody had heard of her. I had no appetite. I was losing weight. Insomnia invaded my life. Whenever it rained, it was Isabel grief-stricken. When the sun shined, it was Isabel wrapping me with her warmth. When it was violently storming, I got slapped with one of her poems. I knew I had to come to terms with the fact that I would never see her again. Reluctantly, I resigned myself to letting go.

It was time to pursue a new life. I became adamant about settling down. Every woman I dated became a candidate for a wife. At that point, what did it matter? As long as she was honest, intelligent, and loved me. I'd marry her. Tolerate her quirks. Bask in her strengths. She didn't have to be perfect. We'd have scores of children and my life would fall into place, a mundane routine as it should be. I'd get up, continue to earn a modest living and return at night and pass time with my family. We'd grow old together through holidays, soccer games, ballet and graduation ceremonies. Relish in weddings and grandchildren. Weather deaths.

And so the rest of my life began: I retired one evening to my study, with the same kind of wine and the same opera I played when I graded Isabel's paper. I sat at my desk and wrote diligently as a naughty schoolboy five thousand times in a notebook, something I would return to time after time throughout my life: *There is no such thing as Isabel B.*

FILM NOIR

You happen to be in a public park and you spot a small child. It doesn't matter if it's a boy or a girl. You look around. The park is desolate, save a couple of school kids wearing winter coats and plaid skirts, backpacks intact, running off into the distance. You make small talk with the small child.

You say, "What a big boy/girl you are to play in the park alone. Although you don't look old enough to play in the park alone. Not this park, not in a city like this. You better come with me—get your thumb out of your mouth—because there are lots of crazy people in this world. I am not one of them." You wonder if this is true. About the world, you mean.

You tell the child to shed trepidation like a snake sheds its jaggy skin. You tell the child you have candy. You take the child by the hand. You talk to it. You say, "What is your name?" But the child is programmed not to tell you. You show the child a picture of your latest. It is a picture of a brick building. The child looks as if he'll/she'll fade-out into the background like in a funky foreign film. You say, "Come with me." Although the child is not programmed to do that, either, it does. Perhaps because of a behavioral malfunction.

The park looks as if it's been shot in black and white. The park is all shadow and drama.

"What does that say on your jacket?" you say. "I don't need reading glasses yet, but sometimes I have trouble with the fine print. What I mean is, I have trouble reading between the lines. Reading between the lines, like fine print, is a suicide note written on eggshells." The child has no clue what the fuck you mean. You sense this. You say, "I mean, reading between the lines is a love note I'll never solve." Still. Your apartment is beyond the park's trees on the other side of the lake. You tell the child to watch its step. "Watch your step," you say. You say, "Do you swim? Do you swim in lakes? I swim, but not in that lake." You are referring to the lake in the park. "That lake is like quicksand." You mean that that lake is deep and deep and deep. "You can't see your toes when you stand, and if you're not standing, well. You can't see anything underneath!" This is what you said. What you meant was: the bottom is muck green. If you stood your feet would go squish into mud. The child drags his/her feet. You say, "Don't drag your feet."

"It's a rare day," you say. What you mean is, it's raw. You mean, it's six degrees, you don't mean not cooked.

Ice coats skinny branches of a tree and frost binds the air. "Look," you say, "those branches are as spindly as a witch's finger and the air, pitch blend, is like the breath that comes out of a witch's head." You mean out of her mouth, not head. Technically, it is the same thing.

It's overcast. It's getting dark. You check your watch and say, "Let me check my watch—it's getting late and it's getting dark. The ground is frozen—watch, don't slip. It's not good when it gets dark not late. It may even be the darkest day of the year! I love years but I hate days."

The child anticipates sweets. Maybe not.

"We'll have you back for supper. Don't tell your mother. I mean, about me, I mean, about the sweets. She might get cross. What I mean is, it might spoil your supper and I'm a stranger." You regret saying this.

"Where do you live?" you say, "there? Or there?" The child must have told you, or, most likely pointed somewhere because you say, "Oh, there." You sigh.

"I've never been over there." You feel something. Envy maybe, because you say, "People who live there wear rubies." You wear fake gems.

Nobody is home at your apartment, but when you say *apartment* out loud you say *flat*. You call it a flat because a flat sounds better. It sounds all Euro. Nobody is ever home where you live—maybe because you live alone. You recollect why. Then you say, "My ex left me last January. He said, *Have A Good Year!* I thought he said, *Wish You Were Here!*" Now solitude makes sense.

You give the kid a teensy pat. "You're a good sport," you say. "If you were an actress/actor I'd give you a part." A part in what you aren't sure.

Finally you're at your apartment, I mean, flat. You search for your keys. It's not in this pocket. It must be in that. There it is. It is poking out from underneath the doormat.

"We must climb those stairs five times," you say. You say this because there are five sets of stairs. Why? Because you live on the sixth floor, duh.

It's almost Christmas and you have no gingerbread. That's because you don't bake. You don't buy gingerbread, either. You ask the child, "What is Santa bringing you this year?" Before the child answers, you say, "Do you want to know what I found under my tree last year?" The child waits. Or doesn't care, either way you say, "Christmas day."

You open your closet because you tell the child this is where the candy is like it's normal to keep candy in a closet. All he/she sees is a row of boxes. "See the boxes?" you say. You don't say, *See the shoeboxes?* because some of them are boot boxes. Which means some held boots once, not shoes. All the boxes contain your best-kept secret minus one. You ask the child if he/she likes lollipops. He/she nods and you ask which flavor. You open a box full of lollipops. (Yes, you really do have a box full of lollipops.) If it's a boy he'll pick orange. If it's a girl, she'll pick purple. That's just the way it is. You think: orange, like your brain, is frenetic. Purple, like images in the Rorschach test, is violent. In short, you are dealing with a child who harbors either frenetic or violent tendencies. Nowhere do you believe color correlates to flavor. You wonder if you are in fact evaluating yourself.

You say, "Let's go home before your mother starts to worry." But the child doesn't want to leave. You don't know this for sure, it's a hunch. You assume the child either a.) doesn't get lollipops at home, or b.) likes you. If you have a low self-esteem you'll circle a.) If you have a high self-esteem you'll circle b.) Maybe it's the other way around.

    The day recoils and closes its eyes. The windows are black squares flecked with light. You are at a loss for what will happen next. You place your ear to the listening: the itinerant wind is lost in the barren city. And you wait.

PUBLICATION NOTES

I am grateful to all the editors who have published the following stories:

"From a Room Above a Mexican Café" *Across the Margin*
"Isabel B." *Able Muse*
"Broken" *Aoife's Kiss*
"Blind Date" *Columbia Journal*
"The Day Before I Died" *Evergreen Review*
"Fast Food Horrors" *Green Hills Literary Lantern*
"Smoking" *Meat For Tea*
"If a Tree Falls" *Pank*
"Nipple Knows Best" *Potomac*
"Prelude to the Afternoon of a Faun" *Foliate Oak Literary Magazine*
"Film Noir" *Sleet Magazine*
"Eight Days with the Yakatori Sisters," *Thema Literary Journal*
***

"Prelude to the Afternoon of a Faun" was nominated for the Million Writers Award and the Pushcart Prize for Fiction

"Blind Date" was nominated for the Pushcart Prize for Fiction and also reprinted in *Flash Boulevard*

"Film Noir" was nominated for a Sundress Best of the Net selection

"From a Room Above a Mexican Café" was listed at the top 20 fiction reads for the year 2020 by *Across the Margin*

Jennifer Juneau is the author of the novel *ÜberChef USA* (Spork Press, 2019) and the full-length poetry collection *More Than Moon* (Is a Rose Press, 2020) which was a finalist in the National Poetry Series. Her poetry and fiction have appeared in numerous magazines such as the *Cimarron Review, Cincinnati Review, Columbia Journal, Passages North, Rattle, Seattle Review* and others. She lives and writes in New York City, and is the curator of a literary series, The Phoenix Poetry Open Mic, Monday evenings in Union Square.

MORE ROADSIDE PRESS TITLES:

By Plane, Train or Coincidence
Michele McDannold

Prying
Jack Micheline, Charles Bukowski and Catfish McDaris

Wolf Whistles Behind the Dumpster
Dan Provost

Busking Blues: Recollections of a Chicago Street Musician and Squatter
Westley Heine

Unknowable Things
Kerry Trautman

How to Play House
Heather Dorn

Kiss the Heathens
Ryan Quinn Flanagan

St. James Infirmary
Steven Meloan

Street Corner Spirits
Westley Heine

A Room Above a Convenience Store
William Taylor Jr.

Resurrection Song
George Wallace

Nothing and Too Much to Talk About
Nancy Patrice Davenport

MORE ROADSIDE PRESS TITLES:

Bar Guide for the Seriously Deranged
Alan Catlin

Born on Good Friday
Nathan Graziano

Under Normal Conditions
Karl Koweski

The Dead and the Desperate
Dan Denton

Clown Gravy
Misti Rainwater-Lites

Walking Away
Michael D. Grover

All in a Pretty Little Row
Dan Provost

These Are the People in Your Neighbourhood
Jordan Trethewey

They Said I Wasn't College Material
Scot Young

Radio Water
Francine Witte

And Blackberries Grew Wild
Susan Mickelberry

Licorice Heart
Miles Budimir

MORE ROADSIDE PRESS TITLES:

Disposable Darlings
Todd Cirillo

Full Moon Midnight
Belinda Subraman

Innocent Postcards
John Pietaro

Cistern Latitudes
James Duncan

Another Saturday Night in Jukebox Hell
Alan Catlin

Abandoned By All Things
Karl Koweski

Ain't These Sorrows Sweet?
Lauren Scharhag

Gregory Corso: Ten Times a Poet
Edited by Leon Horton

She Throws Herself Forward to Stop the Fall
Dave Newman

We Don't Get to Write the Ending
Aleathia Drehmer

These Many Cold Winters of the Heart
Ryan Quinn Flanagan

Things You Never Knew Existed
Josh Olsen

MORE ROADSIDE PRESS TITLES:

Green Roses Bloom for Icarus
Hiromi Yoshida

Let the Scaffolds Fall
Shaun Rouser

Apocalypsing
Jason Anderson

Failing to Fall
James Griffin

Milton Keynes UK
Ingram Content Group UK Ltd.
UKHW041506240924
448733UK00001B/24